Randall Vande Water (signature)

Millennium Memories

**Personalities,
Places &
Pleasures
In the Life of Holland, Michigan**

Color House Graphics Inc.
3505 Eastern Ave. S.E.
Grand Rapids, MI 49508

Cover design and text by Randall P. Vande Water
655 Maple Creek Drive, Holland, MI 49423
Photographs from collections as noted
Typesetting, cover and page composition by Bernard Wright, Holland, MI 49424
Printed by Color House Graphics, Grand Rapids, MI USA 49508

ISBN 0-9652488 3-6

Millennium Memories

Personalities,
Places &
Pleasures
In the Life of Holland, Michigan

By Randall P. Vande Water

FOREWORD

Millennium Memories, in a vivid pictorial display, unrolls images of Holland Michigan's more than 150 years.

This book provides for readers of all ages an intimate view of life in this community. Not designed to specifically trace the chronological development of Holland, *Millennium Memories*, through Personalities, Places and Pleasures, concentrates on presenting examples of life during the second half of the 19th Century and throughout the 20th Century.

Although an historical perspective is woven throughout the publication, the book's purpose is to provide entertainment or reference, nostalgia or enlightenment as it depicts segments of life illustrating and relating to Holland's daily life.

Regardless of prior knowledge of the community, whether native or recent arrival, the reader is exposed to an unfolding panorama of the development of an area. Through the photographs the reader determines the lifestyles of not only Holland's pioneers but also its residents as the community responded to national, state and local responsibilities.

From farm to factory, resort to recreation or agriculture to zoo, readers discover and enjoy these human interest vignettes, depicted as they occurred on the land or waters of this particular place.

Dr. Albertus Christiaan Van Raalte founded Holland Feb. 9, 1847. He died in Holland November 7, 1876 at age 65.

Holland has advanced into an urban center, recognized for its diversity in culture and commerce. More than 350 pictures capture the flavor, the faces and the changing cultural and commercial tastes and fashions of the times as Holland moved from the windswept forested swamp chosen by Dr. Albertus C. Van Raalte Feb. 9, 1847.

Proud of its heritage, Holland is built on a solid foundation of religion and education, a combination that has unlocked doors to the world and given the increasing populace a particular pride.

Through this book's unique format, readers witness mundane and major events. Holland's most famous festival, Tulip Time, is pictorially recorded during the fete's seven decades.

Read the captions, smile or brush away a tear in memory of the past. Remember, life is a scrapbook of history and should be preserved.

Millennium Memories provides preservation.

On Saturday May 15, 1976 Holland welcomed President Gerald R. Ford. It was the first time a U.S. president had visited here while in office. Ford, with a Dutch cap in his hand, waves goodbye before boarding a helicopter at Tulip City Airport. The president, his wife Betty, daughter Susan and U.S. Rep. Guy Vander Jagt rode in an open top presidential limousine in the Parade of Bands.

DEDICATION

To my parents, wife, children and grandchildren

Parents

William H. and Kitty A. Vande Water

Wife

Mary Elizabeth Vande Water

Children

Nancy Ann Vande Water Sivertson
Eric Jonathan Sivertson
Kathryn Lynn Stam
Kenneth Mark Stam
Karen Beth Martinie Stam

Grandchildren

E. Jonathan Paul Sivertson
Kristina Hope Sivertson
Sarah Kathryn Sivertson
Marissa Elizabeth Padding
Alexandra Kendall Stam
Nicole Elizabeth Stam

ACKNOWLEDGMENTS

For more than 150 years Holland, Michigan and its personalities, places and pleasures have been recorded.

And as the world concludes the 20th Century, through *Millennium Memories*, a portion of this community's daily life passes pictorially on these pages.

Thousands of photographs tell Holland's story. A few choices were easy and obvious. Certain pictures provided historical recollections, never to be forgotten. Others were significant by the subject portrayed. Still others were selected, strictly because of their charm. And the final section, Tulip Time, unique first to Holland, Michigan, must be included in any local publication.

Selecting more than 350 pictures from a personal collection was difficult but enjoyable. My wife Mary Elizabeth and I could have chosen another 350 and found the images equally entertaining and informative, but these are our choices. Our assignment was enhanced by the use of some pictures that appeared first in *The Holland Sentinel*, thanks to publisher Ron Wallace.

My parents, the late William H. and Kitty A. Vande Water, saved a variety of pictures. In addition to family snapshots, photographs were also found that were used to illustrate articles written by my father during a 60-year newspaper correspondent career.

Also received were photos from some of Donald L. van Reken's previous publications, plus people have donated pictures or provided information. They are Mrs. Peter (Yvonne) Jonker III, Ernest Penna, Joel Le Fever, Lawrence McCormick, William Plomp, Janice Van Lente, Lucille Donivan, Margaret Van Vyven, Kenneth Zuverink, Harry Daubenspeck, Dianne Moker, Fred Bulford, Mary Dyke, Mrs. John (Mary) Vande Wege, Tino Reyes, Hennrietta Veltman and Frank Moser.

Resources were obtained from Herrick District Library, the Joint Archives of Holland and the Holland Historical Trust.

My wife Mary gave candid comments concerning content and never wavered in her encouragement.

Bernard Wright supplied professional counsel, computer knowledge and technical expertise.

Thanks to these people. And compliments to those readers who have included previous publications on your bookshelves. We hope *Millennium Memories* will be added.

Personalities

This is part of the crowd of 5,000 people at the Holland Pere Marquette train depot Friday, Oct. 25, 1940, to bid farewell to Holland's Co. D of the 126th Infantry. The troops left for Camp Beareguard, La. at 10.15 p.m. The troops had marched from the Holland Armory over Eighth Streeet to the depot. Citizens lined both sides of the street along the line of march, and several marched along the street beside the guardsmen. Saying goodbyes are (center) Cpl. Clarence (Babe) Kuhlman and Wanda Stanisz, the future Mrs. Kuhlman. At far left is Pfc. Osborne Vos; Sgt. Homer Lokker is at right foreground. Also at right in the cap is Henry (Peenie) Rowan, who in 1941 was given a captain's commission to lead the Holland home guard unit. Company D was leaving Holland for a year's military training. Little did this unit of three officers and 77 enlisted men realize that the company flag would fly many places before the end of World War II, Aug. 14, 1945. During this period, this unit as part of the 32nd Division, saw 654 days of combat. Of the original company leaving Holland, nine men were killed in action, one was killed in a military airplane accident and 11 were wounded in action. Throughout their stay, Holland men fighting in the Southwest Pacific, first at Buna, New Guinea, were ravaged by malaria, blackwater fever, tropical ulcers, high temperatures and malnutrition.

Almost 36 years from the day Lt. Col. Matt Urban checked out of an English hospital to rejoin his men at the Normandy, France fighting front, President Jimmy Carter draped the Congressional Medal of Honor around Urban's neck. The president made the presentation in Washington July 19, 1980. Mrs. Urban is at right. This supreme tribute to valor made Urban the most combat decorated sol-

dier in World War II. He had 29 other combat medals and medals of valor from France and Belgium. Seven times wounded, Urban spent 20 months in front-line action in six major battle campaigns in Algeria, Tunisia, Sicily, France and Belgium. While convalescing from wounds, he heard about his unit's losses in France. He voluntarily left the hospital, hitch hiked to the front at St. Lo and retook command of his company. Urban came to Holland in 1974 as City Recreation and Civic Center Director. In September 1980 the street leading to the DAV hall and West 48th Street was named Matt Urban Drive. He retired in 1989 and died March 4, 1995 at age 75. He is buried in Arlington National Cemetery.

Dr. Henry Ter Keurst, who became pastor of Trinity Reformed Church in 1930, served in the U.S. Navy from 1942-44. He was commissioned a lieutenant and served as hospital chaplain in the Aleutian Islands. While on leave, Ter Keurst viewed the names of his parishioners who were serving in the armed forces around the world. Ter Keurst died Nov. 10, 1950 at age 57. Ter Keurst, who graduated from Hope College in 1914, received an honorary Doctor of Divinity degree from his alma mater in 1940.

These G.A.R. (Grand Army of the Republic) hats were worn by members of the Women's Relief Corps, a group of Holland women who were relatives of Civil War veterans who were members of the A. C. Van Raalte Post 262 of the G.A.R. Cornelia (Kate) Van Lente, (inset) born in 1878 and died in 1901 of tuberculosis, was the daughter of veteran Johannes Van Lente. The G.A.R. Post in Holland was formed July 17, 1884 with 23 original members. A youngster, carrying his U.S. flag, marched in step Memorial Day, May 30, 1912 with Civil War veterans on River Avenue near Centennial Park.

Pvt. Johannes Van Lente of Holland served in Co. I of the 25th Infantry Regiment in the Civil War from Aug. 14, 1862 to June 24, 1865. At age 12 he came to the United States from Zwolle, the Netherlands, June 1, 1847 on the Albatross with his parents and three brothers, three sisters and a sister-in-law. Johannes was 27 when he enlisted in the Army. Following the war he was a carpenter and gardener for the City of Holland. He helped design the park's stone fountain. He died Sept. 10, 1911 at age 76.

When Holland Co. D, 126th Infantry officials said Sgt. Arthur (Bud) Woltman could not leave his sit-down strike duty in Flint, Jan. 15, 1937 and return to Holland for his scheduled wedding, he called his bride Frances Annesley. His fiancee drove to Flint with her sister and brother-in-law and were married with military pomp by the National Guard chaplain. Attending were several hundred fellow guardsmen in a dingy room that formerly was a junior high school assembly hall, where Holland troops were stationed. The picture circulated worldwide. Clippings of the photograph, including one from Cairo, Egypt, are in Mrs. Woltman's scrapbook. Following rioting, troops stayed in Flint 36 days to preserve peace prior to the strike settlement.

Private Charles Hiler of Holland, who served in the 105-day Spanish-American War, wore his full battle gear posing at the E.J. O'Leary Studio. Hiler and his brother, Cpl. William Hiler, as members of the 33rd Regiment of the Michigan Infantry, participated in the battle for the city of Santiago, Cuba July 1-17, 1898. Most of the Holland volunteers served in the 32nd Regiment and remained in Florida but did not see combat.

These 43 Central Building School youngsters were sixth graders in 1891. Left to right starting at top row: Louis Van Schelven, Jerry Leapple, Walter Vander Haar, Joe Vork, John W. Kramer, Jean McKay and George Pessink. Teacher Reka Ver Beek, John Ostind, Mable Harrington, Carrie De Feyter, Mary Steginga, Jenny Ver Schure, James Kroorkes, Anna Alberti and Superintendent S.E. Higgins. Jeannie Mulder, Anna Zulusky, Anna Mulder, Hattie Ten Cate, Anna Vandenberg, Norma Anderson, Minnie Reidsma, Minnie Beeuwkes, Anna Van Ry and Wilhelmina F. Schoon. Helen Astra, Anna Ver Hulst, Helen H. Markham, Miss De Kraker, Anna Prakken, Minnie Bird, James Seery, Anna Verhey, Lemma Mokma and Helen Winter. John

Steffens, John Winter, Jacob Ver Schure, Bert Smith, Henry Naberhuis, Egbert Winter, John Dinkeloo and Robert Koeman. The school at the corner of 11th Street and Columbia Avenue (257 Columbia Avenue) has been called Lincoln since June 12, 1915 when all five of the elementary schools were given names of men. The other names and locations were Central, East 10th Street between Central and College Avenues, (Froebel); Maple Grove, 36 East 24th Street, (Longfellow); Van Raalte Avenue, 461 Van Raalte Avenue, (Van Raalte) and Maple Avenue, 156 West 11th Street (Washington).

Graduates of Holland High School in 1890 were Marie S. Damson, Jennie De Vries, Nettie D. Huntley, Beatrice L. Kimpton, John A. Elenbaas, Gerrit Steketee, Anthony Van Ry, Lou E. Markman, Nella Pfanstiehl, Henrietta Van Den Berg and Alice M. Purdy. J.W. Humphrey was superintendent and principal was Miss Delia Cook.

Antje Herremina (Anna H.) Van Lente and Anthony Van Ry were married June 27, 1895. The Boston Photo Co. of Holland recorded the scene. They were married 42 years and spent most of their married life at 201 West 15th St. When they were married, Anna was a bookbinder and her husband, a furniture factory worker. Van Ry died Oct. 10, 1937 and his wife died Nov. 19, 1953.

Bows were popular for young girls in the first decade of the 20th Century as shown by Janet De Graaf who posed with her mother, Mrs. Mary De Graaf.

Sisters (left) Cornelia (Kate) and Johanna Sophia (Jennie) Van Lente were photographed on Feb. 13, 1901 by E.J. O'Leary in his 13 East Eighth Street studio.

Brothers William H. and Bernard Vande Water, dressed in their Sunday finest including bows for ties, posed with their dog Shep around 1908. William was born Aug. 17, 1901 and his brother Bernard Oct. 6, 1903. They lived at 178 East 13th Street, now site of the Hope College Dow Health and Physical Education Center.

Five women composed Holland High School's first graduating class June 27, 1873. Left to right are Alida Binnekant, Nellie Wakker, Johanna Koning, Kate G. Ledeboer and Kate E. Garrod. This commencement was 25 years after the organization of the Holland Public Schools.

E.E. Fell (left) served as Holland Public Schools' superintendent from 1910-1945. This photo marks the renaming of Holland Junior High, built in 1923, to E.E. Fell on May 2, 1955. The building houses Central Administration at 372 River Avenue. J.J. (Jock) Riemersma, (right) was Holland High School principal from 1919-1957. He started teaching mathematics at HHS in 1915-16, and spent two years in the Army during World War I. Riemersma died Nov. 14, 1964 at age 75. Hope College conferred an honorary LL.D. degree on Fell in 1935. He died June 30, 1958 at age 84.

The 1939-40 Holland High School Student Council, led by Mayor Ray Serier, met in the school library.

C.O. Schaap delivered milk in his Riverview Dairy wagon more than 70 years ago. His telephone was 4110 - 4 Rings. The dairy business was active in Holland for many years. The 1940 City Directory lists nine dairies. Several Schaaps were in the dairy business.

Veteran barnstorming pilot Robert Vande Water, flying his red, single-engine, two-seat open cockpit biplane to open Tulip Time, dropped tulips, attached to tiny parachutes, over the City Hall May 15, 1937 in honor of Mayor Henry Geerlings and city officials. Called a "Tulip Time Salute," the occasion also marked the opening of Park Township Airport. Vande Water took off from the airport, which held its dedication with an Air Fair on May 20. Works Progress Administration (WPA) funds paid ($24,500) for most of the 80-acre airport.

Lambertus Tinholt, letter carrier for rural route No. 10 delivered his mail this way Nov. 14, 1908.

Holland pioneer businessman James A. Brouwer, who owned a furniture store bearing his name at 212-214 River Avenue, purchased the 1925 Detroit Edison Electric Car that year and drove daily for a quarter of a century to and from home at 54 East 12th Street to work. He steered with a stick instead of a wheel. His top speed was 20 miles an hour. He changed the car's batteries after traveling abut 65 miles. Brouwer died at age 96 in 1950 and the car is in an auto museum in Flint.

In 1927, through the efforts of Holland City Mission founder Nellie Churchford, the Holland masons and carpenters were among workers who donated their services to construct the building. This picture shows Miss Churchford with the carpenters and the Holland Bricklayers Union No. 19, who built the walls. The $35,000 for the edifice was collected in a two-year fund drive. It was dedicated Sunday, Oct. 16, 1927.

This is a hobo near the Waverly railroad yards in Holland during the 1930s.

Nellie Churchford founded the Holland City Rescue Mission in 1903, a year after she began tent meetings. Miss Churchford died Dec. 6, 1931 at age 57. About 2,500 people attended her funeral in the mission at 178 Central Avenue including the masons, carpenters, plasterers and other workers who had donated their time to construct the $35,000 building.

Gerrit J. Diekema received a Scouting award prior to leaving Holland for the last time Oct. 31, 1930. He became officially U.S. Envoy Extraordinary and Minister Plenipotentiary to the Netherlands following an Aug. 20, 1929 appointment by President Herbert Hoover. Diekema died Dec. 20, 1930 while serving as U.S. Minister to the Netherlands. His flag-draped casket was returned to New York on the steamer *Deutschland* and arrived by train at the Holland Pere Marquette depot Jan. 3, 1931. Two days later more than 3,000 people crammed in Hope (Dimnent) Memorial Chapel for funeral services. Dr. William Arendshorst is the Boy Scout in front.

In April 1939 Woman's Literary Club president Mrs. Kenneth (Margaret) De Pree (left) and Mrs. Joseph (Troupe) De Pree burned the 1926 mortgage acquired during Mrs. Rhea's 1926 presidency to create the Tea Room. The clubhouse, (inset) owned and operated by the WLC until the mid-1990s, was dedicated in 1914.

Holland's first woman jury said "guilty" March 4, 1919 in a "chicken case" in which a woman (Mrs. Elizabeth Gilmore) was convicted of slander following a story about a stolen chicken. A month later the decision was upheld in Ottawa County Circuit Court. Left to right jury members were Jeanette Mulder, Mrs. William (Margaret) Olive, Mrs. Egbert E. (Elizabeth) Fell, Mrs. Frederick (Anna) Aldworth, Mrs. William (Helen) Wing and Mrs. Charles (Elizabeth) Drew. Standing are Police Officer Peter Bontekoe, Justice Thomas Robinson, Prosecutor Fred T. Miles, Daniel Ten Cate and Clarence Lokker, who represented the defendant. The verdict was announced one day before Holland women would vote for the first time for school commissioner. Of 1,033 registered women voters, only 208 voted. But men voters were "less than one in five."

These are not bobbies from an English police force but Holland policemen in 1912. The kettle-like helmets were standard equipment. Frank Austin, Dave O'Connor, Jack Wagner, Cornelius Steketee and Simon Meeusen are standing left to right.

Holland firefighters douse water on the La Barge Mirror Company building on March 31, 1976.

Rose McCormick, an 18-year-old 1945 Holland High School graduate, and her fiance Pvt. Donald Milewski, 19, a 1944 HHS graduate, were kidnapped a day following a Dec. 20, 1945 murder near West Olive. The pair had been forced by hitchhiker and Army deserter Robert Smith to drive them from Grand Rapids, where the couple had been Christmas shopping, to Gary, Ind. They were released unharmed and are telling their story in Holland to Ottawa County Coroner Gilbert Vande Water, State Police Sgt. Vern Dagen and Sheriff William Boeve. In the back are Holland Police Chief Jacob Van Hoff, state police trooper and Holland Police Lt. Ernest Bear. Smith murdered Ray Beh, prominent Grosse Pointe Farms resident and was committed to the state hospital for the criminally insane in Ionia. Miss McCormick and Milewski, who was on military furlough, later married. Everyone in the picture is deceased.

10

Holland's sewer construction gang between 1915-1920. Foreman John Dogger is at right.

City employees are digging a water line on 10th Street just west of Maple Avenue in the early 1920s. The former Anton Seif brewery is the background.

Blueberries were picked by all ages, including migrants and teenage youngsters, when the sandy soil crop needed harvesting in the early 1950s.

This is a group of braceros attending a session in the South Olive Christian Reformed Church at 6200 120th Avenue in the late 1940s and early 1950s. Braceros were used to pick crops including pickles and blueberries.

11

On Christmas Eve, 1940, Women of the Salvation Army Home League in Holland were busy sewing clothing for European refugee children, victims of Nazi Germany in a war that began Sept.1, 1939. Three cartons of clothing, made over from old clothes, had been sent to London, England where the Salvation Army was caring for thousands of refugee children. Included in the clothing sent were 100 pairs of mittens, 30 skirts and sweaters, 50 baby garments, quilts, boys' pants, shirts and overalls. The league was also making over clothing for Holland residents.

Contributions to the Salvation Army's kettles has been a Christmas tradition for more than a century.

In Holland the morning ritual is called the "koffee kletz" and men have gathered in downtown Holland for years. This group is in the 28 West Eighth Street restaurant, called Glatz' in the 1950s, and now named Windmill. George Zuverink, (right) was pitching for the Detroit Tigers in 1955 when he joined the group. Seated from left are Harry Glatz, Harold Oostendorp, unknown, unknown, Dick Boter, Marvin C. Lindeman, Charles Cooper, Charles Madison, Al Piersma and Zuverink.

These patriotic fishermen posed in 1889 when the U.S. flag contained 42 stars.

Two years after riding in the Holland Tulip Festival Parade of Bands as President of the United States, Gerald R. Ford returned as grand marshal. Former First Lady Betty Ford watches as the former Fifth District representative (Ottawa and Kent Counties) struggles with his sweater.

The Southside Industrial Park was the first project for the Holland Economic Development Corporation (HEDCOR) and signage told the story. In 1963 HEDCOR directors campaigned to raise $250,000 for industrial development. Seated from left are Clarence Jalving, Stuart Padnos, Nelson Bosman and C. Neal Steketee. Standing are William H. Vande Water, George Heeringa, Russel Klaasen, Ab Martin, Jay H. Petter, Henry S. Maentz, Henry Steffens and Roger MacLeod.

Willard C. Wichers, with his wife Nell, received an engraved plaque, *A Mill for Bill* from Windmill Island Director Jaap de Blecourt a decade ago. Wichers was honored for his work from 1962-1964 in obtaining an authentic, historic windmill from the Netherlands. The windmill was shipped to Holland and dedicated April 10, 1965. It has been Holland's chief tourist attraction for more than 30 years. Wichers died May 18,1991. Called Mr. Holland for his variety of civic duties, Wichers not only directed the Netherlands Information Service in Holland, he was also longtime secretary of the Hope College Board of Trustees. Hope conferred an honorary L.H. D. on Wichers in 1979.

Hope College Dean of Men, later Dean of Students, Milton(Bud) Hinga digs the first shovel of dirt for Kollen Hall on the southwest corner of 13th Street and Columbia Avenue Oct. 21, 1955. Behind Hinga are Dr. John A. Dykstra, Hope College Board of Trustees president; Dr. Irwin J. Lubbers, Hope College president; Dr. John R. Mulder, Western Theological Seminary president and John Adams, Hope College student body president. The dormitory, which housed 300 men, opened in 1956 and was the first men's dorm on the campus. Hinga, who died May 31, 1960 at age 59, came to Holland High School in 1923 from Kalamazoo College and remained eight years. Beginning in 1931 he taught history and coached at Hope College. He retired as basketball coach in 1948, but remained Director of Athletics. He was Dean of Men 12 years and in 1956 became Dean of Students.

On Aug. 10, 1941 Charles R. Sligh Jr. of Holland won the national water ski championship on Lake Macatawa. Lyda Mae Helder of Holland (Mrs. Morris (Mike) Skaalen) won the women's title. National men's and women's tournaments, sponsored by the Macatawa Bay Yacht Club, were also held here in 1946 and 1947. Sligh's son Robert won the men's crown in 1947. That year Robert teamed with Irene Boer of Holland to win the doubles competition.

For many years, especially in the 1930s, 40s and 50s, Casey Landman, in the sailor cap, operated his boat Sea Foam II from in front of the dock at the south corner of the channel wall at Macatawa Park. The pickup point was east of the U.S. Coast Guard station when it was located on the south side of the channel. Riders were taken into the channel to the north and south breakwater piers where Holland area residents and tourists, with their bamboo poles, would catch their limit of perch. People also fished from the dock at the south edge of the channel.

Queen Beatrix of the Netherlands, and her husband, Prince Claus, visited Holland June 26, 1982. They rode in a carriage with Holland Mayor Richard Smith.

Undefeated world's heavyweight champion Rocky Marciano trained in Holland in 1953. On May 15, 1953 he knocked out Jersey Joe Walcott at 2:25 of the first round for which he received $166,038. The champion returned to Holland in the Holland Furnace Company land cruiser and rode in a convertible in the Saturday Parade of Bands. He retired undefeated in 1956 after 49 victories. He was killed in a small plane crash Aug. 31, 1969 hours before his 46th birthday.

Pottawatomie Chief Simon Pokagon, who died Jan. 27, 1899, spoke in Centennial Park marking Holland's 50th anniversary in 1897. Pokagon, who first visited Holland in the 1860s, lived in Lee Township in Allegan County. Speaking about the remains of an Indian cemetery located on the south shore of Lake Macatawa (site of H. J. Heinz today), Pokagon said: "For the good of yourselves and your children, you had better erect some simple monument over their remains and engrave thereon, "An unknown Red Man lies buried here." (Bones were removed during excavation in 1907.) Pokagon is buried at Rush Lake, near Hartford.

Henry Vander Linde directed Holland Christian High School bands for 36 years, beginning in 1950. He has directed the Holland American Legion Band since 1966, lifting the baton for the 50th anniversary and the 75th anniversary of Holland's community band. The Legion band began in 1920 and Vander Linde is the eighth director.

Places

After a V-shaped split, near the center of the hold of the Burlington, left the ship helpless off Ottawa Beach, the winter ice coated the 268-foot vessel. While buried in the sand, part of the ship's cargo was removed by crane. The ship eventually broke up and sank north of the breakwater about 400 feet off Ottawa Beach. Capt. Everett J. Clemens, commander of the Holland Coast Guard, led the rescue of 24 men in 14-degree temperature off the freighter Dec. 6, 1936. Clemens and three Coast Guard crew members made four trips in a lifeboat over the treacherous water to retrieve the sailors. The crew, including Walter Van Oosterhout, 22, of Holland, were all pulled to safety by 6:30 a.m. A pounding Lake Michigan and low water level caused the Burlington to run aground at 3:55 a.m. during a blinding snowstorm. Clemens said the ship "broke her back" and suffered a jagged hole extending from the deck to the water line. The keel was split a little forward of midship. Loaded with 2, 217 tons of pig iron, valued at $50,000, for the Holland Furnace Company, the Burlington smashed into a five-foot sand-bar. Attempts to refloat the $125,000 ship were futile. Scuba divers have recovered pig iron ingots in recent years.

With the City Hotel and its balcony in the right foreground this is Holland in 1875 looking west on Eighth Street. The two-story Nathan Kenyon building (center) was the opera house. Following an 1877 fire, the McBride building was constructed by attorney Patrick H. McBride and Hope College professor Dowe Yntema. It is now Reader's World at 194 River Avenue. On the left front is Lumblatt's Saloon, Van Duren's building, a fence which guarded Mrs. Koningsburg's flowers, followed by her husband's, Charles Koningsburg, Germania House (hotel), Kuite's meat market, Pete Brown's saloon and the Vander Veen hardware store.. The Hummel Tannery smokestacks, on the southeast corner of Eighth Street and Pine Avenue, which later burned, are in the background. They are not the Cappon-Bertsch Leather Company. Eighth Street (inset) looking east from River Avenue in 1884.

Changes on Eighth Street occurred during the summer of 1974 as the street took on the look of a mall with cutouts for trees and flowers. When completed, one-way traffic rode from west to east from River Avenue to College Avenue. In 1988 Streetscape and Snowmelt were installed with trees, plantings, lighting and brick walks. Snowmelt was an underground heated water plan to keep the sidewalks and streets dry. When completed, one-way traffic from College Avenue to River Avenue went east to west.

The Cappon-Bertsch Leather Company, founded in 1857 and destroyed by fire in 1871, formed a corporation in 1875 and built this facility at the corner of Eighth Street and Maple Avenue, present site of the Civic Center. Manufacturing harnesses and saddle leather, the firm used 100,000 hides and 30,000 skins annually.

18

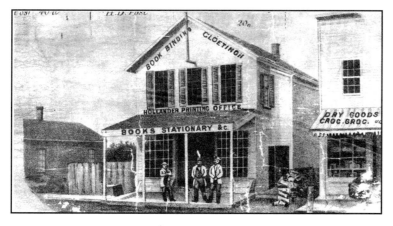

John Binnekant, who arrived in Holland, March 17, 1847 with Teunis Keppel and Wouter Vander Haar, built this store on the northeast corner of River Avenue and Eighth Street, site of the Tower Clock building. Binnekant saw the economic value of the buildings that had been left at Point Superior in 1839, and lugged the lumber on a raft to Holland where he built a hotel. He salvaged some of the timbers for his store. He owned Holland's first newspaper, *De Hollander*, and published it in his store. He also established a bookbindery and bookstore. He reprinted the *History of the Reformation* and *Church History*. (By 1870, after "some economic reverses Binnekant finally succeeded," the *City News* wrote in his eulogy when he died Feb. 7, 1876.) However, the newspaper noted "the great fire of Oct. 9, 1871 left him penniless." He had erected another building at the time of his death. A foundling, Binnekant was raised in an orphanage in the Netherlands and came to Holland at age 38. He first formed a partnership with Willem Houtkamp in 1848 and built the first grocery store "at Black Lake," close to where the River Avenue bridge is today. Binnekant was one of four contractors to build the first bridge. He also served as Holland Township clerk and treasurer and assessor of the school district.

Third Reformed Church was organized in 1867 with the Rev. J. V. Vander Meulen serving until 1871. This wooden building was destroyed in the 1871 Holland fire. The present church stands on the original site on the corner of 12th Street and Pine Avenue.

The Coatsworth House, on the southwest corner of Washington Avenue and Ninth Street, (236 West Ninth Street) survived the Holland fire. The mansard roof is a distinctive trait of French Second Empire architecture, a rarity in Holland. Henry D. Post, and his wife the former Anna Coatsworth, arrived in Holland in 1848. Her family may have moved here later and built the home. Still standing, the home is being restored.

Frequently, farm folk obtained supplies from a traveling merchant who carried his wares in a horse-drawn wagon in the early 1900s.

Teams of horses brought bark down River Street for use at the Cappon-Bertsch Leather Company in the early 1880s. Destroyed by fire in 1871, the plant had been rebuilt by 1875.

With the City Hotel at left and looking east from Eighth Street, Holland was rebuilding after the 1871 fire.

Civil War Holland in 1864 shows River Street looking north, intersected by Eighth Street. On the right are Vander Veen's Hardware, now Baas' and H. D. Post's store, now the Model Drug Store. On the left was the hotel, now Reader's World.

Looking west on Eighth Street in the late 1880s, The steeple is the No. 2 Fire Station at 106 East Eighth Street.

Scott's Hotel stood on the northwest corner of Ninth Street and Columbia Avenue. Located a block west of the depot, the hotel was frequented by train passengers. William J. Scott and his wife, Blanche, opened the hotel in 1877. They came to Holland, before the 1871 fire, from New York where they had lived along the Erie Canal. W.J. died Nov. 20, 1904 and Mrs. Scott, Aug. 29, 1913. The hotel was turned into a rooming house for Hope College students in the early 1900s and was demolished for a parking lot in March 1989.

Constructed by William Kellogg in 1872, the City Hotel stood three stories with a balcony on the second floor. The capacity was 50 guests. Silas, believed to be Holland's first African-American resident, served as the hotel's "bus driver." He said he came to Holland June 7, 1873.

Members of the combined veterans' group started an Avenue of Flags in Pilgrim Home Cemetery in 1984. U.S. casket flags were donated by more than 350 families of deceased Holland veterans.

This liitle girl, with a wide-brimmed summer straw hat, stands in amazement as she looks at the U.S. flags and patriotic bunting on the windows and door of the Jas A. Brouwer furniture store on River Avenue in the early 1900s. The bunting was placed to celebrate the Fourth of July.

E. F. Sutton became Holland's beer baron in 1874. In addition to the brewery business, Sutton's Saloon was located on the southeast corner of Eighth Street and Central Avenue. In this photo taken in the mid 1880s, when Sutton's Saloon was purchased by Arend D. Bosman for a second hand store, the building was moved on the clay and gravel road to East Eighth Street. The two-story building was moved on heavy rollers, (placed under the building at the rear and then carried to the front again.) Participating on the moving rig were Civil War veteran William H. Finch, who fired the Centennial Park cannon every July 4, Art Drinkwater, Frank Stansbury, Hank Lindemeyer, Jake Dogger, Bill Van Anrooy and Adsel Gale, who owned the horse that turned the apparatus that moved the house.

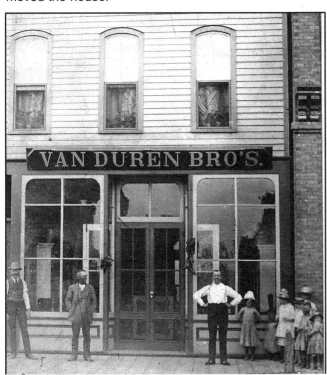

In 1884 the Van Duren brothers, helped by neighborhood children, posed proudly in front of their store. The store at 24 West Eighth Street sold boots, shoes and rubbers.

Opposite Heber Walsh's drugstore on East Eighth Street was C.A. Stevenson's Jewelry Store at 24 East Eighth Street. The 1894 City Directory ad said Stevenson's had a "splendid stock of watches, diamonds and silverware. It pays to know what you are buying. Our guarantee goes with all sales."

A century ago Holland had a downtown Last Resort saloon and a pool room. Situated on Eighth Street near the train depot, the Last Resort signified the last chance to get a drink before getting on the train. On another window the words the First Resort appeared, indicating the closest opportunity for a drink for disembarking passengers.

Owner Peter Brown (left) stands in front of his saloon at 14 West Eighth Street about 1885. At that time River Street was the east-west dividing line and the saloon was just east of River. Brown would never allow a "drunk" in his place. If a man "in his cups" came in, he would simply say, "I dank you got enough" and the customer knew it was time to walk out. Brown was born in Sweden in 1848 and arrived in America in 1870. He came to Holland in 1871 and in 1874 married Miss Ebba Lundblom, a native of Sweden. Brown supported funds for city improvements and was liberal in contributions to public and private charities.

This may be Pete Brown's saloon or one operated by Cornelius or David Blom. E.F. Sutton had a billiard hall license in 1892. Other 19th Century saloonkeepers were Robert Hunt, Charles J. Richardson and William Boyd.

Simon Sprietsma, and his son Nicholas, operated a shoes and rubbers store in 1915 at 28 West Eighth Street. The store's founder, father Lucas Sprietsma's store was located on East Eighth Street in 1894. Around 1885 he was doing business at 18 West Eighth Street.

In the early 1900s Marine Bishop and Warner Alofs owned the bicycle shop on the southwest corner of Ninth Street and River Avenue. They repaired sewing machines, grapho-phones, lawnmowers and sold bicycle and motorcycle tires. They also sold cigars. By 1915 Peter Raffenaud owned the business with Bishop.

Walsh Drugs, DuMez, Lokker-Rutgers and Nies Hardware were among the stores on Holland's north-side of Eighth Street between Central and College Avenues. Walsh started on the site in 1885 while DuMez came in 1903. Lokker-Rutgers occupied the property since 1892 while Nies Hardware was there in 1895.

Two merchants, wearing hats, lean up against counters in one of Holland's downtown general stores a century ago.

This gentleman posed with his horse and milk wagon in front of the Herman Prins Garage located at 160 East Eighth Street more than 50 years ago. The Holland Rusk Company, site of the U.S. Post Office since 1987, is in the background.

In 1919 Simon Pool, assisted by Ryne Visser, operated a downtown grocery and meat market. The lady and child are Mrs. W. G. Hoogendoorn and daughter Alice. In 1915 Pool operated the Holland Packing House Market at 208 East Eighth Street.

The Pere Marquette Railroad had two tracks in front of the depot in the early 1900s.

An early photograph, during the 1870s of the Chicago and West Michigan locomotive.

The Chicago and West Michigan Depot, Holland's second, faced east in 1895. It was in the center of the Allegan Y track. Muskegon and Grand Haven trains came from the west over a curved trestle crossing the Black River near Central Avenue at Fourth Street. After loading, trains would "Y" onto the Allegan division. Telegraph operators stood under the canopy. Twenty passenger trains arrived and departed daily.

Railroad workers stand next to Engine No. 37 at Holland's first railroad station around 1880.

Mrs. Anthony (Anna) Van Ry was proud of her two-porch home at 104 East 16th Street in 1903. Her children, Franklyn, with tricycle, and Kathryn (Kitty) were dressed for the occasion.

Erected in 1899, (top) the Holland factory, of the Holland-St. Louis Sugar Company, was a joint effort of Holland businessmen and farmers. Because of the farmers' success raising sugar beets in the early 1900s the company paid $5,000,000 for beets, $500,000 for labor, $700,000 for supplies and manufactured more than 176,000,000 pounds of sugar. Farmers and their trucks (bottom) are lined up Oct. 18, 1938 on West 14th Street waiting to deliver sugar beets. The company closed in 1939. The office was at 345 West 14th Street, present Community Action site, and the plant was along Kollen Park Drive. The factory building was demolished in 1984.

A home at 958 South Shore Drive, built by George Poole of Chicago, served as the Sunnycrest School for Girls from 1924 until 1936. Founder Miss Helen Clark, who had outgrown her facilities in Chelsea, Mich., selected Holland. "The home was for girls ranging from 5 to 15 years, whose start in life is for some reason cramped by unfortunate circumstances," the Holland City News reported. Called Windy Ridge, the John Sexton family lives in the home.

Lake Macatawa ice was harvested March 7, 1921 for use in Holland ice boxes. E. Lugers is at left. A. Neerken, on the right, is pushing the ice to the wagon. Adrian Heneveld is on the wagon putting cakes in place. They are working at Jenison Park, a block east of Easter Marina. It is now the home of the Tiara Yachts Corporate Yachting Center on Lakeway Drive.

With snow piled on both sides, workers and interested bystanders stand next to an Interurban railroad car near the Sunnybrook Station on the Holland to Saugatuck route. The photograph was taken near Eugene Teusink's farm following a 1910 storm that made traveling difficult for the Grand Rapids, Holland and Lake Michigan line. At the time of the storm the name Chicago had replaced Lake Michigan.

Located near 160th Avenue in Virginia Park between South Shore Drive and 32nd Street, the Interurban car barn was used to repair trains on the Grand Rapids to Saugatuck line. These are 1915 pictures in the second car barn. The original car barn, containing ten cars and a snow plow, burned Jan. 10, 1900.

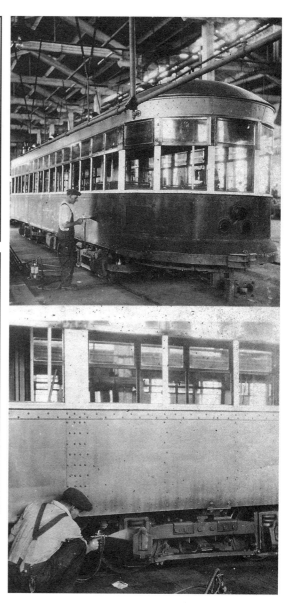

These men built the Bush and Lane Piano Company at 171 East 24th Street. Hyo Bos at left was the foreman and John Dogger is marked with an x. Grand, upright grand and player pianos were manufactured here between 1905 and 1933 in the 300 by 65-foot two-story building, with basement. The company came here under the Bonus Plan that provided five acres of land. (Under the plan the factory received an inducement - building, property, something tangible. The property deed was held by the Bonus Committee so that if the concern was a failure the committee still had the building and property which could be offered as an inducement to another firm.) The Great Depression was the plant's demise. Baker Furniture acquired the building in 1933 and later enlarged the facility which is just west of the Pere Marquette Railroad track.

Workers constructed the Medusa Portland Cement Co. silos in 1939. They were located at the foot of Graham Avenue and the Docks, one block north of West Eighth Street. Prior to the silo construction, the Graham and Morton Transportation Lines docked at the foot of Graham Street. The silos were demolished Aug. 21, 1999.

The Lake Macatawa and Black River waters were dredged in mid-July 1938. In December, 1939, sand and dirt were trucked in for landfill near Third Street and Pine Avenue, prior to the construction of the new Holland Municipal Power Plant which was completed and opened in 1940.

Constructed of Waverly stone in 1892 as a bank, the tower clock building was getting a facelift in 1923. Harry Padnos, who sold clothing, hats, caps, gents' furnishings, boots and socks is next door at 188 River Avenue.

The Holleman-De Weerd Ford Auto Company and garage was at 23-25 West Seventh Street in 1924. On display are two-door Model Ts, four-door Model Ts with different style roofs and a Lincoln. This was one of the first of the auto dealers in Holland. Seventh Street was red brick.

The William Brusse Co. was located at 194 River Avenue on the southwest corner, site of Reader's World book store. In the 1894 City Directory the ad states the owners were "merchant tailors, clothiers and men's furnishers." A cartoon angel character carried a sign reading: "the latest in sack coats" next to a sharply-dressed man wearing a derby. Dr. Abraham Leenhouts had his office upstairs. Nick Dykema, who also did tailoring, rented the facility and sold clothing for several years, starting about 1911.

The Holland Furnace Company office building and gymnasium on Columbia Avenue, near 20th Street, in the early 1920s. To the left is the YMCA building which the furnace company used as a dock. In Holland from 1906-1966, the firm came here under the Bonus Plan. The office building, now Black River Charter School, was built in 1930 at 491 Columbia Avenue. The company also built the Warm Friend Tavern, now Resthaven Apartments at 3 East Eighth Street, which opened in April 30,1925 and remained a hotel until 1981.

This was a reading room for Warm Friend Tavern guests when the 144-room facility opened in April 1925.

The Warm Friend Tavern kitchen staff posed in the mid-1930s. The Tulip Room, one of Holland's most popular banquet places, was the dining place

not only for hotel guests but visiting dignitaries, service clubs, college parties and wedding receptions.

Started by Phillips Brooks in 1934, the 7up Bottling Company of Western Michigan was at Fourth Street and River Avenue in 1940 and stayed in this location until moving to the Southside Industrial Park more than 30 years ago.

The Hotel Macatawa, completed in the spring of 1895 and pictured in the 1930s, gave Macatawa Park a luxury hotel. Built by the Macatawa Park Company, the facility was acquired by the Macatawa Resort Company and its president, Swan Miller, who was the largest stockholder. The 115-room hotel accommodated 250 guests and the dining room had a 300-seat capacity. Miller came to Macatawa from Chicago in 1891 when he retired from real estate. A Civil War veteran, he died in 1941 at age 98. Simon Den Uyl purchased the resort and hotel from Miller's niece, Georgia Miller, in 1945. More than 50,000 meals were served in 1955. Den Uyl's son, Dick, demolished the hotel in 1956 because costs to modernize were prohibitive. The Point West Restaurant and Motor Inn opened on the site Feb. 24, 1965. The restaurant, no longer a Den Uyl property, was torn down in the early 1990s.

Photographed from the dock, this is the Waukazoo Inn in the late 1940s. The veranda (inset) was a popular place to relax. Famed attorney Clarence Darrow visited in 1932. He was the guest of Pulitzer Prize winning author Charles Edward Russell. Boat motor magnet Ralph Evinrude was a 1940s visitor.

Opened in 1902 and followed by a 60-room addition in 1912 to accommodate 125 people, the Waukazoo Inn was on Indian Point on Lake Macatawa's northside. The hotel was razed in the spring of 1960. Real estate developments resulted in the building of permanent homes throughout the peninsula.

This is a 1923 photograph of the 10th hole at the Holland Country Club. The HCC marked its 75th anniversary in 1997.

Castle Park was built in the 1880s by Michael Schwarz of Chicago. Located between Holland and Saugatuck at the western end of 145th Avenue, the Castle is several hundred yards from Lake Michigan. A tailor, Schwarz came to Chicago from Germany and became wealthy in real estate. In 1893 the Rev. John Parr of Chicago found the abandoned castle and used the facility for his prep school summer camp before becoming a full-time resort operator in 1896. His nephew Carter P. Brown bought the facility in 1917 and the Brown fami- ly ran the Castle for more than 50 years. Stone for the tower came from the Waverly quarry east of Holland and 17-year-old Cornelius Knoll chipped away at blocks of stone to form the curve of the tower.

Tunnel Park is an Ottawa County park. On Lakeshore Drive, the tunnel looked like this a half century ago. It is located in Park Township. Park, formerly a part of Holland Township, became a township in 1916.

WPA workers, beginning in 1935 and continuing through 1938, built and improved the oval at Holland State Park. The federal grant totaled $31,000. Also built was a combination toilet-bath house. The 1937 attendance reached 1,300,000.

The old Macatawa pier around 1900 attracted both men and women for fishing. The lighthouse (right) at the end of the pier was constructed in1872. During the building of this breakwater, which was completed in 1905, six people drowned. Four men perished Nov. 21, 1906 during a storm when they were repairing the pier.

This life saving station along the channel on the south-side of Lake Macatawa at Macatawa Park began in 1886 and the U.S. Lifesaving Service opened on the south channel wall in 1893. This service later was called the U.S. Coast Guard and that station was built (above) on the south channel wall in 1903. It was torn down in the 1960s. The present Coast Guard station, on Lake Macatawa's northside, opened June 16, 1955. The southside site was purchased by the US. government in 1873 from Henry D. and Anna C. Post for $200.

Forty years ago Ottawa Beach drew all ages of sun bathers in many varieties of regalia.

From the Holland Harbor Lighthouse Holland State Park looked like this in June 1987. The beginning of the Spy Glass housing development is noticeable in the distance.

Hope's Carnegie Gymnasium stood from 1906 to 1982. Andrew Carnegie gave Hope College $30,000 to construct the building. Part of the DeWitt Center is now on the site.

Holland's familiar water tower landmark on West 28th Street between Washington and Van Raalte Avenues was built (inset) in 1937. Opened in December, the 108-foot tank was erected for $42,000 and had a 500,000 gallon capacity. The tank rested on 10 piers, nine outside and one inside. Each pier supported 485,000 pounds of weight. It was dismantled in the 1990s and the space was used for Habitat for Humanity housing.

With soldiers, army airplanes and the 121st Field Artillery Band playing in front of a crowd of 3,500 people, U.S.31A was dedicated Aug.11, 1936, just south of 28th Street and Michigan Avenue. The road was 8.3 miles of paved concrete and became the new highway between Holland and Saugatuck, now called Blue Star Highway. With a 120-foot right of way, the highway had a 62-foot grade and a 20-foot concrete pavement.

The River Avenue bridge nearly a century ago when it was called the old Grand Haven Road and bridge.

Established in 1926 by the Vandenberg Brothers Oil Company at 1649 West 32nd Street (corner of 160th Avenue and 32nd Street), the Windmill Station pumped Van's Gas. This road, now 64th Street, was known then as the West Michigan Pike from Holland to Chicago.

This sign greeted residents, visitors and tourists to Holland and its cobblestoned Pine Avenue prior to World War II.

This wooden shoe sign greeted Holland residents and visitors on West 16th Street in the 1930s.

White's Market at 236 River Avenue placed these hams in their window prior to the 1916 Thanksgiving. Holland Furnace employees were given coupons to redeem at White's for the holiday hams. The turkeys were "special fed" according to owner Thomas White.

A glass negative reproduction of a windmill, barn, and couple in a buggy around the turn of the 20th Century.

Agricultural agent Ira Krupp marks a corn test plot in a rural field near Holland for the Ottawa County Extension Department in May 1991.

Two-story Washington Elementary School, 156 West 11th Street, was constructed in 1926-27. An open house was held May 24, 1927.

Dedicated June 7, 1929 in the presence of the General Synod of the Reformed Church in America, Hope Memorial Chapel's cornerstone was laid Oct. 12, 1927. On Aug. 14, 1959 the Board of Trustees named the chapel in honor of former President Edward D. Dimnent (1918-1931) who died July 4, 1959.

St. Francis de Sales Catholic Church and School at Thirteenth Street and Maple Avenue was completed in 1923 and the parish school began that year in Sept. It was conducted by the Sisters of Mercy. The school closed at this location in 1999. The first St. Francis Church at 360 West 20th Street was dedicated Aug. 7, 1903. The brick is now on a home at 461 Harrison Avenue.

Lugers School pupils stand in the doorway in 1935. The school was part of the Ottawa County School System. Students attended through the eighth grade. Upon graduation they were promoted as freshmen at Holland Junior High School. The school, at 752 Lugers Road, was annexed to the Holland school district in 1959 and renamed Lakeview Elementary School. Neighborhood students attend from kindergarten through fifth grade and then enroll in Holland West Middle School.

Holland High School's dome fieldhouse (inset) was constructed in 1961 and play began in1962.

Torn down in 1985 for the site of Evergreen Commons, Holland Christian High School was built in 1923 for $90,000. Twenty-nine 1924 students were the first graduates and commencement was held in the gymnasium. The building was later used for a junior high when a new high school opened at 950 Ottawa Avenue in 1968.

A crane, aided by an iron line placed around a damaged engine, was used following a train accident near the Walsh-De Roo Milling Company which opened on East Seventh Street in 1882 and made Sunlight Flour.

A severe December blizzard damaged five schooners in 1873 and the ships were driven ashore at River Avenue and Third Street where they remained until spring.

Macatawa Park fire April 18, 1925.

Fire in 1956 destroyed the Red Brick Tea Room, 294 River Avenue, featuring tourist rooms and owned by Joseph and Grace Kooiker. Herrick Public Library opened on the site May 7, 1960.

The Holland Fire Department, under Fire Chief Cornelius Blom, and members of the Board of Police and Fire Commissioners, pose with their trucks and equipment in front of the City Hall in the mid-1920s.

Potter's Field (below) in Pilgrim Home Cemetery on the north side of East 16th Street contains remains of unidentified and identified people. On July 2, 1941 the body of Willard L. Carson of Liberty, Ind. was exhumed. Carson, while living in a rooming house in Holland, drowned in Lake Michigan between Ottawa Beach and Eagle Crest. The FBI and Indiana authorities identified the remains through fingerprints and the body was reburied. Carson had been wanted for the 1926 murder of four people, including two officers. Ottawa County Coroner Gilbert Vande Water is standing at left.

Holland moved its boundaries in 1958 increasing the size of the city and school district to six miles.

Built as a WPA project, Holland's police station and one of its two fire stations served the community more than 40 years. New police and court buildings were constructed in 1972.

Windmill Island is at right foreground while a large ship is docked in Lake Macatawa near the James De Young Power Plant on a summer August evening in 1983.

Concrete seating is erected at Holland Municipal Stadium for a September 1979 opening.

On May 15, 1971 the Holland Jaycees sponsored a fly-in at the Tulip City Airport.

Main Street Director, now Assistant City Manager, Greg Robinson, handled the development of Streetscape and Snowmelt (above) in 1988. Eighth Street from 56 West Eighth Street, west of River Avenue, to 106 East Eighth Street, east of College Avenue was torn up. Trees, plantings, lighting and brick walls constituted Streetscape while Snowmelt, built at the same time, provided an underground heated water system that keeps the Streetscape sidewalks and street dry during a snowfall.

Construction started on Herrick Public Library in 1959. It was dedicated May 7, 1960. Forty years later an addition was completed and dedicated June 19, 1999.

Centennial Park added brick pathways in May 1987. Bricks were purchased by residents in a buy-a-brick campaign. Councilman and future Mayor Philip Tanis spearheaded the program. Mayor William Sikkel is at right and Forrest Fynewever, who suggested the bricks, is in the center.

Quonset buildings for public housing occupied the parking lot in 1950 of the future site of the Civic Center.

Soon after the Civic Center opened in October 1954, concerts, commencements, religious services and Tulip Time events filled the arena. The city purchased the land in 1941 and began building construction in 1952.

The McLellan five cent to $1 store at 2-4 West Eighth Street is in the left hand corner of this early 1950s southside of Eighth Street picture. Visible is Central to River Avenue as seen from the sixth floor of the Warm Friend Tavern at 5 East Eighth Street.

General Electric was welcomed to Holland April 1, 1955. Less than a

year before, the company started building its Hermetic Motor Department building on East 16th Street, west of U.S. 31. At the dinner Holland Evening Sentinel publisher W.A. Butler presented Ab Martin, GE manager, with a bound copy of newspaper stories concerning GE's move to Holland. The other GE hermetic motor plants were in Fort Wayne, Ind. and Tiffin, Ohio. The dinner at Hope College's Durfee Hall was sponsored by the Holland Chamber of Commerce and Holland Township, where the GE plant was located. Martin wore a Dutch costume for the event. Standing are Henry Ter Haar, Chamber president, Walter Vander Haar, Holland Township clerk and H.A. MacKinnon, GE vice president. GE stayed in Holland more than 30 years.

After Thanksgiving Day shoppers filled West Shore Mall in 1990.

Holland State Park, with Mount Pisgah at left, the channel and Lake Macatawa more than 35 years ago.

The all-steel fishing tug, built by the Chambers brothers, Clifford, Lloyd and Murray, in 1944, passes the lighthouse on its way back to Lake Macatawa following a 1960s daily expedition for lake trout and chubs. Commercial fishing ended in 1976 when the Michigan Department of Natural Resources forbade commercial fishing south of Holland. The brothers sold their boats in 1976.

Great Lakes freighter enters Lake Macatawa after clearing the Holland Harbor channel in the early 1950s.

Loading scrap metal for an overseas shipment to Japan in 1961 was the *S.S. Zermatt*. The Greek ship was docked at Harrington Coal Dock and carried compressed auto bodies to Japanese smelters. Also on board, which went through the ship's hatches into the hold, were misshapen girders. The *Zermatt* was one of the foreign ships that made Holland a port.

Meteor, a whaleback tanker, unloaded its cargo in 1948. The last of this type of U.S. registry, the ship was a frequent visitor during the season to deliver gasoline.

During the 1990s the lake freighter *Wolverine* passes Kollen Park after unloading at the Holland port.

Holland Community Hospital opened Jan. 21, 1928 (inset). Several additions have been made to the facility, starting in 1948. This aerial picture was taken ten years ago. The latest addition opened in May 1998.

In October 1990 pre-schooler Emily Apple learned from an emergency room nurse what occurs during an examination at Holland Community Hospital.

Pleasures

Regardless of age or apparel, tent camping at Holland State Park at Ottawa Beach always attracted boys and girls. These campers were part of the oval crowd more than 50 years ago. Establishing a temporary clothes-line for hanging bathing suits and towels still is a camp site priority. Beach outfits, camping conditions and tent varieties have all changed but during summertime, "livin' is easy" and the state park continues to lead Michigan in attendance every year. Ottawa Beach has been a state park since 1927. When the facility opened as a state park, there was a shortlived move by Holland residents to name the park "Wooden Shoe." Parking and camping space remains a problem. In 1965 the state park was enlarged east of Ottawa Beach with the purchase of 90 acres on the northside of the Ottawa Beach Road. Formerly the nine-hole Ottawa Beach Golf Club, the property housed the Ottawa Beach Cabins owned by Martin and Kay Michielsen. That October the state paid the Michielsens more than $127,500 for the property which included the shoreline south of the highway. The acquisition more than tripled the size of Holland State Park.

The original Ottawa Beach Hotel was two stories and built on a hillside in 1886. It's first name was The Ottawa. Since then the area has been referred to as Ottawa Beach. An 1897 Atlas lists the adjacent area as Park Ottawa West.

The first Macatawa Park Hotel was completed July 1, 1882 and J. W. Scott was the first manager. J .R. Kleyn was the architect for the building which was started that spring, a year after the Macatawa Park Association was formed. In addition to the corrugated roof, the hotel featured boardwalks.

Having added a second smokestack the *City of Holland* is docked 90 years ago at the Graham and Morton docks, just west of the West Michigan Furniture Company. The ship was launched April 10, 1893 and sailed between Holland and Chicago for more than 35 years. Her sister ships were the *Puritan* and the *City of Grand Rapids.* Owned first by the Holland & Chicago Transportation Company the ship was later purchased by Goodrich Lines, who later owned the Graham and Morton Line.

One of the ships making trips to Chicago from Holland was the *City of Holland.* Passengers used the Interurban or a ferry boat to get to the ship docked at Macatawa Park before World War I. The Ottawa Beach Hotel is in the background.

Post Boy was one of the several ferries operating early in the 20th Century from the various resorts. The boat burned in August 1905.

Lady Hamilton was sailing Black Lake Aug. 19, 1910.

Organized in 1899, the Macatawa Bay Yacht Club built this facility on Lake Macatawa in 1939. Fire, believed started in the dining room, destroyed the clubhouse July 4, 1963. The $150,000 loss was partially covered by insurance. A new clubhouse was commissioned July 27, 1964.

This is the stairway to the cottage "Sign of the Goose" at Macatawa Park where L. Frank Baum, author of *The Wizard of Oz*, lived from 1905 to 1909.

Angel's Flight, a cog railway up a Macatawa Park dune, opened Aug. 14, 1909 and prospered 13 years. Two cable cars were electrically controlled from the park's pavilion. The inclined railway was 190 feet long with two cable cars, one descending and the other ascending. They ran on a 45 degree slope between the waiting station at the top and the pavilion. It was advertised to be 225 feet to the top.

This auditorium at Macatawa Park was completed in 1910 and torn down in 1926. The first auditorium was completed in July 1892. Seating 3,000 people and 160 by 125 feet, it was located on a leveled off sand dune at Crescent Park and torn down in 1910.

These are Interurban riders who visitied or worked at Jenison Park and Macatawa Park in the early 1900s.

This is an Indian camp south of Holland in 1890.

Holland High School's 1912 football team, coached by Charles (Cubby) Drew won four of six games and outscored the oponents, 90-26. They posed in front of Holland High School on Graves Place, later called Horace Mann Junior High and East Junior High. The team defeated Hope College twice and South Haven once, split with Grand Haven and lost to Grand Rapids Union.

The 1911 Holland High team posed in a studio and several wore their headgear.

54

While John Buchanan of Holland was patenting his aeroplane, this airplane proved a local spectacle in 1913. An airship, called "The Flying Machine," arrived in Holland July 31, 1913 and participated in an air show at the Holland Fair, site of the southside of Pilgrim Home Cemetery. On Aug. 13, 1913 aviator E.O. Weeks astounded churchgoers at 9:30 a.m. when they saw his aeroplane about 4,000 feet up over the partially completed new high school on West 15th Street.

Here is Ottawa Beach in 1923. It became a 32-acre state park in July 1927.

Dedication of the Holland airport in 1929 at the northwest corner of 136th Avenue and Riley Street featured a Ford Trimotor plane. This is the present site of West Ottawa High School.

Women wearing fancy flowered hats certainly attracted Holland men before World War I.

Bathing beauties were posing for tin types in 1900.

Three lassies prepare for a quiet boat ride on Lake Macatawa in the early 1920s.

This quintet of Holland belles, wearing their finest beach wear, are ready for a boat ride in Lake Michigan about 1910.

A century ago Macatawa Park bathers enjoyed a bathhouse on Lake Michigan.

The Johannes and Jantje Van Lente family posed in 1907 with grandparents, parents, children and grandchildren. Abraham Lincoln's portrait is on the wall. From left to right: Bottom row: Adeline Vander Hill, Janet De Graaf; Middle row: James Vander Hill, Geneva Van Lente, Jantje Bouwman Van Lente, Kenneth Van Lente, Johannes Van Lente, Franklyn Van Ry, Anna Van Lente Van Ry, Kitty Van Ry. Top row: Ralph Van Lente, Jennie Van Lente Vander Hill, Mary Van Lente De Graaf, Anthony Van Ry, Johanna De Cook Van Lente, Frederick Van Lente, Earl Van Lente, Gertrude Riedsema Van Lente, Edith DeGraaf Boylan.

Brother and sister Franklyn and Kitty Van Ry study their music before their piano lesson in 1910.

The big swing, roller coaster and visits from elephants made Jenison Electric Park an exciting amusement place. Opened in 1892 the amusement park was started in 1903. The roller coaster was a popular attraction, opening in 1908. The park continued until the demise of the Interurban in 1926.

A balloon flight, featuring a specially attired entertainer, attracted a number of Holland men around the turn of the century.

Winter in downtown Holland in the early 1900s brought out Holland's "first trailer" on wooden sled pulled by three mules. The trailer was standing at the southeast corner of Eighth Street and Central Avenue. Jon Boone, Leon Reeves and Bill Bosman are riding the mules. Hub Boone's livery was across the street, then called Market Street. A sleigh is at left. Buildings are the City Hotel and the First State Bank, which started in 1889 and moved into this building in 1894.

"*I've Been Workin' on the Railroad*," was the song these fellows enjoyed as they took a break and enjoyed a drink. Their task was repairing the railroad tracks in Holland more than 75 years ago. Or with the horse and cut timber visible, they may have been lumbermen who were relaxing on the railroad equipment.

Teams of horses lined up on Eighth Street, East of Central Avenue, are pulling two circus wagons and a water wagon in the early 1900s.

Getting dressed up and relaxing with a bottle before Prohibition.

Celebrities or politicians may have ridden passenger trains that passed through Holland and the crowds turned out. Famed orator and presidential candidate William Jennings Bryan visited Holland and Hope College four times between 1900 and 1924. On Oct. 10, 1900 Democratic candidate Bryan's campaign special train stopped in the railroad yards and Bryan spoke from a furniture truck owned by the West Michigan Furniture Co. Their secretary-treasurer was George Hummer who admired Bryan and introduced him here. This may have been part of that crowd.

Holland's martial band, which met once a year on Memorial Day and then participated in the event, posed for this picture in 1935 in Centennial Park. Organized in 1886, the fife and drum corps group's two original members pictured were shaking hands, Ben Mulder (left) and Cornelius Dalman. In the front row are Mulder, Dalman, Peter De Kraker and Jacob Steketee. Back row: George Dalman, Clifton Dalman, Edward P. Stephan, Anthony Van Dort and Peter Steggerda.

These happy fellows played in the Holland Concert Band, probably after the 1904 Citizens Concert Band.

On June 16, 1904 the Citizens Band was organized in Holland and presented summer lawn concerts.

A contemporary popular vocal musical group, the Holland Chorale, directed by Calvin Langejans, annually performed concerts and a Tulip Time production following rehearsals like this in August 1991 at Camp Geneva.

Juvenile Drum Corps posed in a Holland park in the late 1920s.

Damson's Orchestra entertained for Holland audiences and Macatawa Hotel guests in 1910.

The Ford Model T was America's most popular car from 1905 through 1927. Holland residents were among the 15 million who purchased a black model. Family or best friends enjoyed rides, provided the tires didn't puncture.

This Model T in Holland carried 1926 Michigan license plates.

Couples courted in a horse and buggy about 90 years ago.

Leonard Kievit of Holland leans on his 1912 model car while a young lady watches from the door.

This 1931 Chevrolet and its occupants were reminded of Holland's snowy winters.

These people are enjoying a boat ride and picnic on Black Lake in 1910 as guests of Albert Meyer, who owned Meyer Music House. Employees and family members attended. Some were identified by the late Marquerite Meyer Prins. "Mart Dykema and his wife are next to my mother - then Wilma Westrate who took care of the barn and horses, then Dad Meyer, Nella Meyer seated in plaid dress, Freddie Meyer, M. Prins, Margie Dykema, Harris Meyer at top and Helen lower down behind Dugan" - the nickname for John Van Vyven, father of Margaret Van Vyven, who provided the picture. "Seated on the edge right - third one is Damson and the man embraced by the gal used to have a furniture store." Others identified were Herm Cook and Ben Sterken. Employees of Meyer's Allegan store are also pictured.

Opened Nov. 3, 1911 the Knickerbocker Theater at 86 East Eighth Street featured a play *Brewster's Millions*. Vaudeville, silent films and local stage productions played to capacity crowds.

The East End Drug Store at 217 East Eighth Street, owned by Hayes J. Fisher, located along the railroad tracks, featured an ice cream soda and provided a backdrop or a stop for this man and his horse and buggy around 1914.

A buggy ride after World War I drew a crowd on the north-west corner of Eighth Street and Central Avenue. Background landmarks are the First State Bank, attorneys Diekema, Kollen and Ten Cate, Green Mill Cafe and the Bob Shoppe.

Hope College Homecoming festivities in the 1920s meant decorating the roadster and filling the rumbleseat while passing the Rexall Store at 194 River Avenue.

Hope College freshmen and sophomores pulled across Black River in the 1917 Tug-of-War. The pull has been a Hope tradition for more than a century.

Ice boat sailing was fast and popular on Black Lake in the 1920s and before.

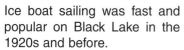

Several of these stuffed birds and animals reappeared in 1998-99 at The Holland Museum as part of the "A Zoo by the Lake" exhibit. George Getz' Lakewood Farm and Zoo was featured. This exhibit, photographed in 1933, was part of Getz' Museum at his facility which closed Oct. 25, 1933. Many Holland residents and tourists visited the farm and zoo from 1910 until it closed.

George Getz' zoo camel defeated a horse and sulky at the 1916 Holland Fair. The fairgrounds are now Pilgrim Home Cemetery on the south side of East 16th Street.

RiRi, one of the lions at Getz Zoo, is coaxed by zoo manager A.M. Peterson prior to the lion's leaving for Brookfield Zoo in Chicago. The lions, elephants, tigers and many other animals, plus birds and other fowl, were part of the nation's largest private zoo during the 1920s. It was located at the west end of Lakewood Boulevard at Lakeshore Drive.

On Wednesday afternoon Aug. 15, 1945, following a spontaneous Eighth Street parade Tuesday night after President Truman's end of the war announcement at 6 p.m., a parade was held, led by the Holland American Legion band, and followed by Legionaires, numerous cars with people on the running boards and fenders, and quickly-constructed floats on trucks. Music was played at Kollen Park and refreshments served to thousands.

The Holland City Band made an impromptu appearance on Nov. 11, 1918 when the Armistice ending World War I was announced at 2:25 a.m. An organized parade began at 7 a.m. on Eighth Street and lasted until 3 p.m. and included floats, factory workers, businessmen, decorated automobiles, trucks, moving vans, school children carrying flags and brass and martial bands.

Civil War veterans, members of the A.C. Van Raalte Post No. 262, Grand Army of the Republic, converged at the corner of Eighth Street and River Avenue in 1890.

The Dye Works float was on Eighth Street in the UWC parade.

A United War Charities parade on River Avenue in 1918.

Holland holds its Decoration Day parade May 30, 1921.

Holland's Martial Band leaves for a G.A.R. Encampment in Detroit in 1910.

The Masons marched downtown in an early 1900s state convention.

Decoration Day, later called Memorial Day, parade lines up at Eighth Street and River Avenue in 1889.

Seventy-five of the 107 Holland children whose tonsils were removed in 1936 received help from the Good Fellows Foundation of the Holland Exchange Club. In the background are (left to right): Jacob Fris, president, Exchange Club; A.C. Keppel, chairman, Good Fellows Foundation; Albert Lampen, secretary, Exchange Club; Alma Koertje, City Nurse; William J. Brouwer, member, Good Fellows Foundation and Paul Hinkamp, secretary, Good Fellows Foundation.

On May 3, 1938 the combined chorus of the elementary, junior high and senior high students of the Holland Public Schools performed in a Music Festival in the Holland High School auditorium at 96 West 15th Street. This building, now used for Community Education, was HHS until the high school opened Jan. 27, 1962 at 600 Van Raalte Avenue.

Speeches made in Centennial Park and a parade through a wooden arch covered with canvas on West Eighth Street, highlighted Holland's 50th anniversary in 1897. Fifty years later in 1947 Mayor Ben Stefffens and Miss Columbia LaVerne Huyser watched while Miss Holland Sally Diekema cut a community cake in Kollen Park. *The Past Is Prologue* pageant was held three nights in Riverview Park and included a re-enactment of the 50th Anniversary with Mrs. Jack (Kathleen) Stroop and Mrs. John (Shirley) Percival dressed in Gay Nineties costumes. R.P. Vande Water was one of the pageant narrators.

Boys and men were required to have shoulder straps on bathing suits at Boy Scout camp on Lake Michigan north of Ottawa Beach in the 1920s.

These swimmers are completely covered in the 1920s. Arrests were made in 1932, citing a state regulation, if men's bodies were bared to the waist or the straps of bathing suits dangled over the shoulders.

Car models have changed, (this is 1922) but the traffic remains clogged, in the more than 75 years that people have been flocking to Ottawa Beach.

In 1935 members of the Holland Fish and Game Club covered the water and used a net to remove bass at the club's pond on M-21 between Holland and Zeeland. The fish were then planted in Lake Macatawa.

In 1935, the same year Black Lake was renamed Lake Macatawa, members of the Holland Fish and Game Club were netting tons of fish from the inland lake. Netting was done in early spring in Pine Creek Bay or the Big Bay and fish were shipped to fish markets in large cities, including New York and Chicago.

This pile of fish was caught through the ice from Black Lake (Lake Macatawa, June 8, 1935) prior to World War I.

Bamboo poles and long sticks were used in the 1950s along the north channel wall to catch fish in Lake Macatawa.

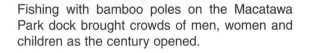

Fishing with bamboo poles on the Macatawa Park dock brought crowds of men, women and children as the century opened.

Fishing along the water's edge at Kollen Park was popular in June 1985.

Fishermen applied sputs to cut through Lake Macatawa in January 1983 while others sat and fished outside a shanty.

A duck hunter takes aim in the Black River marsh 40 years ago.

Pheasants were first planted in Ottawa County March 27, 1895. The county and northern Allegan County became two of the biggest ringneck hunting areas in Michigan and the midwest as evidenced in this early 1960s picture. A decade later, for several reasons, including hard winters, end of the soil bank and pesticide DDT, local pheasant hunting ended.

Practicing archery in 1939 at Harrison Avenue and 20th Street were from left Neal Houtman, Isaac (Ike) De Kraker, John Vande Wege and Don De Kraker while four future Nimrods watched attentively. One boy had a coin changer, often used by youngsters delivering newspapers.

Horse shows were staged at the Castle Park and Waukazoo resorts in the early 1930s. The shows continued after World War II and later were held at other locations near the resorts.

On March 31, 1946 Holland enjoyed a spring day and these Holland High School students rode in a convertible enjoying the weather and celebrating the school's victory in the Michigan Class A State basketball tournament. Arlene Poll drove her passengers Elaine Brower, Betty Gilcrest, Carol Houtman and Esther Huyser. Riding on the running board of the other car are Robert (Bud) Miedema and Eugene Van Dyke.

Holland sports fans were standing in line to purchase tickets for a high school basketball tournament game in the mid-1940s.

A forest of masts as sailboats sit anchored at Macatawa Park 15 years ago.

More than 40 years ago at Kollen Park Dad was teaching the youngsters how to fish and wait patiently.

For children staying in a trailer at Holland State Park the slide was as popular as Lake Michigan.

This is 1897 Ottawa Beach when the postcard manufacturer spelled it Ottowa and the residents sought federal funds to improve the pier.

Relaxing, picnicking or watching sailboats and power boats in the Holland Harbor channel always wiles away time. Similar scenes never change, as proven on this 1986 Labor Day weekend.

Sailboat racing, whether 60 years ago or today, looks the same and Lake Macatawa challenges young and old sailors. Jimmy Brooks, Jim Boter and Hadden Hanchett, sailing in this sloop, combined to win the Hobeck gold cup and the Seagull trophy in the MBYC Labor Day races. In a June 30, 1946 C scow race, contestants Del Van Tongeren, William Baker, Bill Lowry Jr., Bob Hobeck, Bob Den Uyl, Bob Sligh, Jack Gogolin and Peter Van Domelen III sailed around the starting buoy.

A pretty girl and a male photographer produced this 1950s sun, sand and Lake Michigan waves picture at Holland State Park. Ottawa Beach led Michigan parks in attendance 40 years ago and still remains the state's most visited park.

MICHIGAN'S MOST SCENIC BOAT RIDE

ON THE WATERS OF

Lake Michigan and Lake Macatawa

TWO HOUR CRUISE

ADULTS:

$1.00

CHILDREN:
(Under 12)

60c

Round Trip

Leaves Kollen Park Daily:

Main Dock at Foot of West 10th Street, Kollen Park, Holland, Michigan

1:00 P.M.
3:00 P.M.
5:00 P.M.
7:00 P.M.
9:00 P.M.

Thru Labor Day—Weather Permitting

THE FERRY BOAT **WOLVERINE** (HOLLAND)

SEVENTY PASSENGERS — GOVERNMENT INSPECTED — DIESEL POWERED

Docks at Kollen Park, Waukazoo Resort, Macatawa Hotel, Ottawa Beach Pier

A Treasure Trip for Camera Fans

You may take pictures of Large Lake Passenger Liners, Oil Tankers, Cement Carriers, Lake Freighters, Palatial Yachts, Beautiful Cabin Cruisers, also Sail Boat Races, Outbord Motor Races, Etc.

You may see Champion Skiers in Stunts, Thrills and Spills; Bathing Beauties and Expert Swimmers along the Shores and Beaches

Michigan Water Wonderland

- - - in all its Beauty

The WOLVERINE will take you along the wooded shores of Lake Macatawa and the white sandy shores of Lake Michigan, also the great and picturesque sand dunes. You will see many nice homes and fine estates, resort hotels and motels, summer cottages and cabins. You will cruise thru the Government Million Dollar Concrete Channel and Breakwater, past the Coast Guard Station, Lighthouse Towers and into the blue waters of Lake Michigan and along shores of Macatawa Resort and Ottawa Beach, one of Michigan's largest Trailer parks and Tented City, out into Lake Michigan, then back to Kollen Park, completing two hours of comfortable relaxing pleasure. Soft Drinks and Refreshments on the boat.

CHARTER PARTIES FOR CHURCHES, SCHOOLS & CLUBS

No Reservation Necessary for Small Groups. Step Aboard, No Ticket Needed

For Further Information See Capt. Ernest Wingard at Boat, Phone EX 2-3385, or Write 244 W. Ninth St.

THE FERRY BOAT **WOLVERINE** (HOLLAND)

Member Holland Chamber of Commerce & Western Michigan Tourist Association

Main Dock at Foot of West Tenth Street, Kollen Park, Holland, Michigan

FREE PARKING AND PICNICKING PRIVILEGES IN KOLLEN PARK

Returning to their winter mooring at the Montello Park docks in the mid-1950s, the *S.S. North* and *S.S. South American* concluded another summer of taking passengers on the Great Lakes. Owned by the Chicago, Duluth and Georgian Bay Transit Company, the ships wintered here from 1914 until 1958. The *North*, sold to the federal government for a merchant marine training ship, sank in an Atlantic Ocean storm off Nantucket Sept. 15, 1967. The *South* made its last trip to Expo '67 in Montreal Oct. 16, 1967. The ship was sold to the Seamen's International Union in 1967 and was first docked in Virginia, and then moved to Camden, N.J. in 1974. Purchased in 1988 by the Kurt Iron and Metal Works of Baltimore, the ship languished in a slip until Aug. 18, 1992 when the rusted metal and rotted wood were junked. For many years the *S.S. Alabama* wintered here. She was stripped and converted into a crane barge in 1961 and still operates in Saginaw Bay.

(Page 80) The ferry boat *Wolverine* continued a service, from the 1940s into the 1960s, of taking passengers to Kollen Park, Waukazoo, Macatawa Hotel and Ottawa Beach that had started in the 1880s.

Dredging Lake Macatawa and near the Holland breakwater in Lake Michigan has been a U.S. Army Corps of Engineers annual ritual. On May 2, 1954 the *Hains* was busy near the pier. Dredging inspector D.C. Frank, boatswain Fred Beaune and deck hand Joe Marsen watch the action. The *Hains* replaced the *General Meade*.

In the early 1960s a group of Holland men, several of whom were immigrants, formed the Holland Hotspurs soccer team and played their home games in Riverview Park.

The Interurbans played softball in Holland in 1910. One player (far left) was Oscar Peterson, later Holland City Clerk.

From 1958 through 1964 in the early 1960s Don Cook of Holland (standing second from left) presented Saturday night basketball in the Zeeland High School gymnasium and the Civic Center (2,857 first game) to overflow crowds. Called Cook's Oilers, the team was composed of former Big Ten basketball stars, plus ex-Hope College, MIAA, Holland and Holland Christian athletes. In 1964 a victory over the Grand Rapids Tackers gave the Oilers the Midwest Professional Basketball League championship. The 1960-61 team was composed of (standing): Warren Cook, Don Cook, Ron Robinson, Tarp London, Paul Benes, Ray Ritsema, Henry Hughes and Coach Gene Schrotenboer. Kneeling are Bud Kendrick, George Duncan, unknown, Steve Cook, Ron (Peanuts) Nykamp, Herbie Lee and Gary Lee.

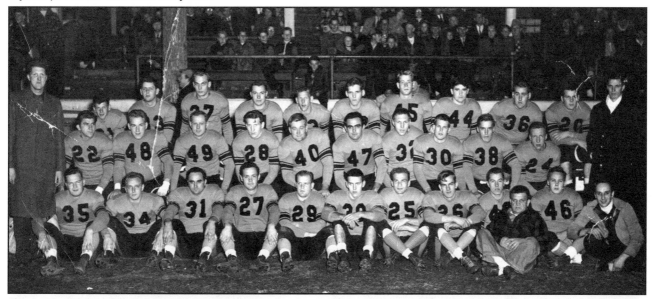

From 1947 through 1949 the Holland Hurricanes played football in the Michigan Independent Football League. Organized and operated the first two years by Fred Bocks, the Holland Lions club took over the team in 1949. Home games were at Riverview Park and more than 4,000 fans attended the first game. In addition to ex-Holland High and Hope College players, the Hurricanes also had former Grand Haven, Zeeland and ex-collegiate players and fielded a 30-member unit. Games were against Benton Harbor, Grand Rapids, Detroit, Jackson, Ann Arbor, Flint and Highland Park.

Baseball games were played at the 19th Street field in the early 1900s. Games were also played on the southwest corner of 16th Street at River Avenue.

Second baseman Harry De Neff models the Holland Flying Dutchmen uniforms in the late 1940s. During the early '40s "Dutchmen" appeared on the uni- form as worn by pitcher Clyde O'Connor. After World War II, for a season, the Dutchmen wore the old English D on their uniforms as they received previously worn white uni- forms from the Detroit Tigers. Business manager Russell Vande Poel arranged the deal. Mike Skaalen pitches in a uniform worn by the 1945 world champion Tigers.

The Holland Independents, this is the 1922 contingent and managed by former Chicago White Sox property Ralph (Babe) Woldring, were the first team to play in Riverview Park in 1918.

Several of these Holland Independents earlier played in the Class D Midwest League during 1910 and 1911.

High school basketball fans filled the Holland High fieldhouse in 1962 to watch the first basketball game in the new facility.

Title IX, approved in 1972, was evident 20 years later as the Holland Christian girls challenged Holland High.

Holland and Holland Christian high school boys became basketball rivals in 1969 and have played each other 30 years.

Rocket football has been popular with youngsters for more than a generation. These 1991 players were coached by Lonnie Haynes (left) and Doug Bazan.

Holland Municipal Stadium opened Sept. 7, 1979. This is a Holland High School game that first season. Athletic teams had played at Riverview Park under a covered grand-stand since Oct. 8, 1932. The grandstand was torn down in 1983.

"confetti in the water pail" prank. Playing for Holland were Gene Schrotenboer, Ken Schippers, both Bob Van Dykes, Frank and Lou Van Dyke, Ken Zuverink, Ron Nykamp, George Botsis, Ron Isreals and Dell Koop. In the preliminary game the Michigan College All-Stars lost to Clarence (Bevo) Francis' Boston Whirlwinds, 91-58. The former Rio Grande (Ohio) College and 6'9" player, Francis made 37 points. Earlier that season Francis had recieved national notoriety, before he was expelled from college for skipping classes, for scoring 113 points against Hillsdale College. The Stars included Ron Bos, Jun Bremer, Jerry Jacobson, Bob Visser, Al Nelson and John Brannock from Hope College, Duane Rosendahl, Calvin; Fred Vander Laan, Ferris and Hess Weaver, Alma. The Civic Center opened officially with an open house Nov. 16, 1954.

The West unit of the Harlem Globetrotters, complete with all of their antics, won an exhibiton (52-27) basketball game against the Holland Stars Tuesday Oct. 26, 1954 to officially inaugurate Holland's new basketball arena, the Civic Center. An overflow crowd of 2,700 fans witnessed the initial contest. The 'Trotters built up a big lead and then began clowning, fancy ball handling and dribbling. The entire fourth quarter featured clowning including the "basketball switch," with a basketball on a string, a "medicine" ball and a "hollow" ball substitute and the

Before the July 4 fireworks were displayed from Kollen Park over Lake Macatawa, Holland families enjoyed the show at Municipal Stadium in 1987.

Hundreds of spectators turned out on the Black River banks for the dedication of Windmill Island April 10, 1965 by Prince Bernhard of the Netherlands and Gov. George Romney of Michigan.

Two Holland girls represented Holland with invitations to several Michigan mayors to attend the Mayor's Night performance of the Hope College stage play *Knickerbocker Holiday* as part of the 125th Anniversary observance Aug. 17, 1972. The ambassadors took with them windmill pins, bags of rainbow colored tulips and a letter from Mayor L.W. Lamb Jr. Invited were the mayors, mayors pro tem or council members. The ambassadors were Cindy Tamminga, a Dutch Dancer, and Estelita Saucedo, the Lation Americans United for Progress queen. Donald L. van Reken was chauffeur.The girls posed in front of the Dutch in Michigan sign in Centennial Park, placed by the Michigan State Historical Commission.

The Nativity scene was an annual attraction in Centennial Park in the 1950s and 1960s. On Dec. 10, 1954 Holland Junior Chamber of Commerce president Arthur Schwartz presented the Nativity to the city. The Jaycees had conducted a fund raising campaign to purchase the figures. About 200 people witnessed the event. Mayor Pro Tem Laverne Rudolph accepted the gift. Ward Wheaton presided and the Rev. Christian Walvoord gave a prayer. Carols were sung by the Christian High sextet, Holland High ninth graders and the Camp Fire Girls. The scene was illuminated every night during the holidays, the lights going on the same time as the street lights.

On January 21, 1967 Holland Harbor and channel were jammed solidly with ice and snow.

Ottawa Beach icebergs were large and exciting more than 75 years ago.

(Inset) All of the public address announcements for the Holland Fair in the 1920s were made from this gazebo. The gazebo is now on the Van Duren property at 99 North 120th Avenue.

Since it began in 1958 the Ottawa County Fair has beckoned young lovers, like this 1971 pair, to kiss at the top of the Ferris wheel.

Three-year-old Brita Jasinki began a love affair with a goat at the Ottawa County Fair in 1990.

A prize Holstein was displayed by this young man a decade ago at the Ottawa Fair.

Roy Walters of Holland loved to spend time on his houseboat *S.S. Royal* cruising through Black River viewing the fish, birds and Windmill Island.

Holland's Window on the Waterfront opened in 1987 with a boardwalk and benches along Black River from River Avenue to Columbia Avenue. *Windmill De Zwaan* is in the background.

Bouws Pool, located west of Pilgrim Home Cemetery on East 16th Street near Fairbanks Avenue, provides hours of summertime fun for Holland youngsters. Given to the city by the Russ' Restaurants' founder the late J. Russel Bouws, the pool was constructed in 1973. Bouws died Aug. 18, 1992 at age 78. These youngsters were swimming in June 1991.

Holland's Municipal Swimming Pool was approved in a millage and opened in 1962 on the southwest corner of 22nd Street and Maple Avenue. A large addition was completed in 1999 on property formerly used for track and other athletics by the Holland Public and the Holland Christian Schools.

Selecting a queen is the highlight of the Latin-Americans United for Progress annual festival. A first weekend in May highlight since 1970, these young women were queens 20 years apart.

Bicycling, whether at Tulip Time in 1969 or anytime, remains a fun activity for youngsters. The old City Hall and No. 2 Fire Station is in the rear along with the Rokus Kanters home at 88 East Eighth Street. Kanters was a successful harbor builder, constructing harbors not only in the Netherlands and Holland, Michigan, but in Galveston, Chicago and Coney Island, New York. Kanters was Holland mayor in 1885-86. His sons were printers, *De Hope* newspaper publishers, hardware store owners, bookkeepers and commercial travelers. His daughter, Jennie, was city librarian.

The Junior Welfare League *Follies* were a winter highlight in the late 1950s. The Civic Center rocked with laughter for the "hula hula" dancers. Proceeds went to Holland children's projects selected by the women's group.

Wind surfing was a 1990s enjoyment as Lake Macatawa breezes helped near the Holland State Park campground.

Field days and track meets, including the high jump, always provided challenges at Van Raalte School in the early 1970s.

Roller blading continues to attract newcomers years after Matt Kling tried this pair.

One of the first sports to try the Civic Center parking lot in the late 1950s were go-carts.

Ice skating on playground rinks brought hours of winter fun more than 30 years ago.

Sledding at Van Raalte Farm hill attracts familes every winter. Purchased by the city in 1983 for $350,000 from Van Raalte family heirs, the farm added the sledding hill in the mid-1990s. Taking advantage of the hill in 1998 are (left to right) Jonathan Sivertson, Marissa Padding, Sarah Sivertson and Kristina Sivertson, along with the Sivertson trio's mother, Mrs. Eric (Nancy) Sivertson. Nature paths and picnic groves are other recent features. The son of Holland's founder, Ben Van Raalte, built his homestead on one hill after the Civil War. Van Raalte Farm is located between East 16th and East 24th streets. The eastern lot line is Country Club Road.

Snow piled high during the winter of 1936 provided man-made hills for children.

Snowsuits kept children warm in 1940.

96

Shuffleboard at the 21st Street courts is especially popular for Holland seniors.

Helping mother at Farmers' Market remains fun like this mother and daughter discovered in 1990 when Virginia Oakley and her two-year-old daughter, Sara, visited the Civic Center parking lot, site of the two-day a week market from May through November.

DeGraaf Nature Center, at 26th Street and Graafschap Road, honors one of Holland's Park Superintendents Jacob De Graaf.

An Ottawa County farmer operated this cornpicker in November 1982.

Tulip Time

It's brotherly love as three-year-old James Vande Poel kisses his older sister, Mary, 5, at the Little Netherlands outdoor exhibit during the 1942 festival. The Little Netherlands, at Windmill Island since 1965, was a miniature Dutch village of houses, churches, public buildings and canals, along with sculptured to scale people, located on the northeast corner of 13th Street and Central Avenue. It was built in 1938 by S.H. (Sipp) Houtman and Louis Mulder. The 1942 Tulip Time, curtailed because of World War II, featured the Russell and Olive Vande Poel family strolling in front of the Warm Friend Tavern. The children are Mary and James walking and Sarah in the wooden cart. Clyde H. Geerlings took the picture which was circulated throughout the nation. The Vande Poels, who owned Superior Sport Store in 1942, still own the store at 202 River Avenue. Because of World War II, Tulip Time was curtailed from 1942 through 1945. The eight-day event became a four-day festival from Wednesday through Saturday in 1946.

Centennial Park tulip beds attract six couples attired in Dutch costumes. These tulips were part of the 50,000 blossoms in the park in 1930. (Inset) Tulip Time's first float in the early 1930s was a log cabin schoolhouse, built for realtor C.C. Wood, 36 East Eighth Street, and pulled by flatbed truck. Dutch costumed children rode on the float.

Thousands of tourists and visitors toured the Nelis Tulip Farms on Lakewood Boulevard prior to World War II. Harry Nelis Sr. started the operation in 1917. Now called Dutch Village, Nelis built his Dutch Market in 1957 and moved the business to (12350 James Street) U.S. 31 and James Street. The former tulip site is now the Bay Meadows housing development.

Lindy gained nationwide fame as the dog that drew the Dutch milk cart in the first Tulip Times through 1937. Owned by the Harry White family of route 3, Holland, the dog was 10 years old when killed June 15, 1937, apparently struck by a car. Purchased for nine-year-old Roy White as a puppy, the dog was named after Charles A. Lindbergh who had just completed his historic New York-Paris non-stop flight in 1927.

As the 1930s dawned, dolls and doll carriages were part of Tulip Time parades. At right are Janet and Jimmy Brooks, the children of the Phillips Brooks of Holland. The elder Brooks was the founder of the Seven-Up Bottling Co. of Western Michigan.

Holland businessmen were the "cleaning crew at the tulip festival" in one of the early festival post cards in the mid-1930s.

Throwing water always has been part of the Volks Parade scrubbing as this 50-year-old picture illustrates.

As part of a pre-Tulip Time 1931 promotion for newsreel cameras, two blocks of Eighth Street were scrubbed with Dutch Cleanser a week before the festival. Holland High School girls, dressed in "Little Dutch Cleanser" costumes and wooden shoes, applied the cleanser after the streets had been drenched by the city water wagon. Scrubbers were Holland businessmen with wide brooms. The scene, complete with the recorded sounds of street babble, were seen the next week in movie theaters throughout the nation. However, because of the residue left on the pavement, the stunt was never tried again. Girls participating were Josephine Kuite, Edna Dalman, Doris Van Lente, Vera Damstra, Ruth Dekker, Marian TeRoller, Olive Wishmeir, Athalie Roest, Jean Rottschaefer and Virginia Kooiker.

Warm Friend Tavern waitresses scrubbed Eighth Street in the early 1930s with kitchen brooms.

Getting a drink from a pail was an extra for this young woman during an early street scrubbing scene.

Crates containing the 1954 shipment of tulip bulbs was received from the Netherlands and opened by city employees.

Thirty years later another batch of bulbs were planted along the eight miles of tulip lanes.

The Tulip Time Band Review in Riverview Park, originated by Holland High School band director Eugene F. Heeter, began in the early 1930s and concluded each year with a massed band performance.

These are 1937 festival spectators.

World heavyweight champion, (1919-1926) Jack Dempsey, visited Holland several times as a guest of Lakewood Farm and Zoo owner, George Getz. In 1930 Dempsey refereed a boxing exhibition in the Holland Armory. Dempsey's final appearance here was May 1, 1962 when he was presented a pair of wooden shoes and entertained with Holland High School Dutch Dancers. He died May 31, 1983 at age 87.

First grade youngsters and their teachers patiently wait for the start of the Children's Parade in the early 1950s.

Parking a 1939 Mercury, adorned with Dutch-costumed children, advertises not only a new car, but also the festival.

Throngs fill the street following the Saturday Parade of Bands after the 1946 resumption of Tulip Time.

In 1971 visiting buses found a parking place south of Kollen Park.

The final pre-World War II Saturday parade crowd.

Two Dutch tots visit with World War II veterans from Percy Jones Hospital in Battle Creek during the 1946 festival. The veterans were recovering from wounds received in Europe. The far right veteran has brought his pre-World War II vintage box camera.

Painting the miniature figures for the Little Netherlands exhibit was a tedious task for these three Holland women in 1938. Results of their work are seen below with the Dutch farmer and his wife, dressed in the Volendam costume, along with their Holstein cow.

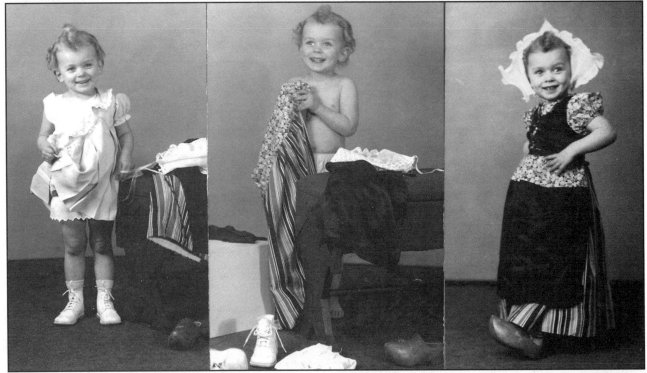

Nina Streur, three-year-old daughter of Mr. and Mrs. Richard Streur, Rural Route 6, Holland, transformed herself from 20th Century America to 17th Century Netherlands in three pictures taken in 1939 by Holland photographer Harold Beernink, who had his studio at 19 West Eighth Street. Nina was chosen by the Tulip Time Committee as one of six Little Dutch Delegates who had been selected to receive the honors given to queens of other festivals. Because of their respect for Queen Wilhelmina, Holland residents in charge of the festival decided they would not institute the custom of having a festival queen. Other Little Dutch Delegates were Sandra Key Decker, daughter of Mr. and Mrs. Jack Decker, R.R. 4; Earl Cranmer, son of Mr. and Mrs. Bert Cranmer, 181 West 14th Street; Herbert Wybenga, son of Mr. and Mrs. Herbert Wybenga, 129 East 18th Street; Judith Ann Rypma, daughter of Mr. and Mrs. Don Rypma, 21 East 13th Street and Emily Vinstra, daughter of Mr. and Mrs. Robert Vinstra, R.R. 2. Tulip Time featured the tots in various parades and as festival Good Will Ambassadors in surrounding cities. They also were used as press photographers' subjects. Their pictures appeared in advertisements and in news stories as the community worked to promote the festival.

Longfellow School sixth graders dressed in Dutch costumes in 1938 prior to the annual Children's Parade. The teacher/principal was Miss Dora Strowenjans. She has displayed the Golden Rule on the wall. Dutch plates were also exhibited. The students were reading *Studies in Conduct*. Students were studying the various provinces of the Netherlands and are dressed accordingly. Included are (left to right): Carl Jordan, Dingeman De Witt, Lloyd Streur, Doris Wieskamp, John Bremer Jr., Don Van Ry, Don Sundin, Ruth Risselada, Steve Covell, Lois Caauwe, Frank Jillson, Doeda Risto, Jack Morerell, Kathleen Kragt, Norm Piersma, James Franks, Arlene Wieten, James Klomparens, Stanley Van Lopik, Melvin Klinge, Faith Den Herder, Mary Van Wynen and Peter Terpsma.

Glamorous motion picture star Dorothy Lamour visited the festival's opening day in 1940. *Grand Rapids Press* correspondent William H. Vande Water is in the background along with Dutch Dancer Joanne van der Velde. The little girls Mary Lou Van Dyke and Mary Lou Buis presented the actress a bouquet of tulips.

Movie stars Virginia Grey, with camera, and Richard Arlen attended Tulip Time in 1938. They enjoyed the opening Saturday's Volks parade and street scrubbing and remained here through the following Wednesday, (above) to watch the Children's Parade. Mrs. August Landwehr, widow of the Holland Furnace Company founder, Mayor Henry Geerlings and Furnace company President P.T. Cheff are also seated. Grey and Arlen stayed with the Cheffs at their Hazelbank estate. Superintendent of Schools E.E. Fell (standing, center with hat) looks at the parade, probably wondering why the two boys in front of the reviewing stand are not in the parade.

George Raft and Faye Wray (left) headed the 1939 movie contingent. They are pictured with Mayor Henry Geerlings, Edmund Lowe and Mary Brian. The quartet were busy producing films that year. Miss Wray starred in the 1933 *King Kong* production. They were brought here by the Holland Furnace Company and presented a nationwide radio broadcast about Tulip Time on the show's opening day, that year, Saturday, May 13.

Michigan Gov. Kim Sigler scrubbed streets in the 1948 festival. He was the first governor to don a Dutch costume and scrub with local politicians and townspeople. Sigler is joined by William H. Vande Water, executive secretary of the Holland Chamber of Commerce.

Gerrit Ten Brink carved thousands of wooden shoes. Ten Brink, 85 in 1943 and a native of the Netherlands, said he once finished 19 pairs of shoes in one day. During World War II Ten Brink was producing seven or eight pairs a day by hand because "klompen" makers were flooded with orders from war plants, acid manufacturers and numerous other firms, as well as individuals' needs for wooden footwear to replace the scarce leather shoes. Each order carried the reminder that wooden shoes do not bend like leather footwear and extra heavy socks were needed.

Promoting Tulip Time resulted in a pre-festival show of scrubbing the street a day prior to each festival. Staged first in 1950, prior to the on-the-spot television cameras, these pictures would serve as "opening day" photo coverage for newspapers and television. The scenes, like these youngsters scrubbing, were shot on Tenth Street in front of the Bell Telephone Company building which displayed Dutch architecture.

From 1949 through 1960 Michigan Gov. G. Mennen Williams attended the opening Wednesday of Tulip Time and scrubbed streets, entertained with Klompen Dancers and posed for amateur and professional photographers. He was an old hand at festival entertaining when he danced with these Holland High School Dutch Dancers, Gloria Hungerink and Connie Du Mond in 1952. (Inset) Television was recording Holland's famed festival in the early 1960s.

The Dutch barrel organ, a gift from the people of Amsterdam in 1947, was a popular entry in the 1950 parade and provided a fine carrier of a group of Holland High School Klompen Dancers. Because the Amsterdam residents were grateful for the financial and clothing help given them by Holland, Michigan residents during World War II, they reciprocated during this community's Centennial Year. The organ, which was refurbished in 1996, is at Windmill Island and is part of the annual festival parades.

Holding a pole helped young elementary school students keep their lines straight on River Avenue in 1950.

Little Dutch girls had priceless expressions a half century ago.

Holland High School senior Dutch Dancers entertained on Eighth Street in 1950. They are Judy Kronemeyer, Donna Tanis, Virginia Koning, Karel-Mari Kleinheksel, De Lene Barr, Anne Beerboom, Jeanne Cook, Myra Saunders, Marianne De Weese, Joan Souter, Jean De Pree and Gloria Bear.

Miss Lavina Cappon, Holland High School home economics teacher and daughter of Holland's first mayor Isaac Cappon, had the final word for Holland High School Dutch Dancers. These girls, wearing Volendam boys' costumes, were inspected by Miss Cappon in 1959.

Maybe the wooden shoes made her feet hurt, but this little girl, decked out in a Middleburg, a Netherlands province, costume wasn't happy during this 1950 festival parade. The pieces of metal are called "kissers" and indicate that the wearer of this cap is not engaged to be married.

Popcorn, with pure creamery butter, from the Colonial Sweet Shop was a must for festival parade watching.

The 12th Street boulevard was a popular spot to photograph these 1950 Dutch-costumed children.

Ken and Kathy Stam pose in Centennial Park in another photo opportunity for parents and tourists in 1969.

Holland High School's marching band does its traditional *Tiptoe through the Tulips* dance every Tulip Time.

The band has been marching in wooden shoes since 1958.

Dutch-costumed children added their charm to the picturesque scene of Windmill Island in 1968. Nancy Vande Water (second from right) and Barbara Miller are dressed in Isle of Marken costumes while John Miller and William Klomparens are wearing Volendam costumes. More than a million and a half people have visited the 235-year-old, 125-foot windmill called *De Zwaan.*

These Dutch costume clad youngsters have learned *Tulip Time,* a song they are singing for festival listeners in 1950. Holland Public Schools elementary vocal music instructor Margaret Van Vyven wrote the song.

For more than a quarter century the diversity in Holland has changed considerably as is evidenced in the annual festival Children's Parade which annually attracts more than 7,000 students from the community's public, private, parochial, charter and home schools. This group is from Washington Elementary Public School. Teachers include Margaret Krause, David Hemmeke, Connie Nieto, Pam Mastos and aide Jackie Tonno. These youngsters marched in 1982.

Ethnic diversity is evident every Tulip Time as this elementary student illustrates in a recent parade.

Nets, containing homemade paper fish, were a Thursday school parade favorite more than 40 years ago.

"Spotting Mom" is this young man's expression in the 1969 Children's Parade. Kenneth M. Stam had constructed his paper tulip, complete with stem and bud, and surely wanted his mother to see him and his parade project.

Riding in a wagon during the 1997 Volks parade was a special treat for three-old twins, Nicole (left) and Alexandra Stam.

This blond Dutch-costumed boy with decorated wooden shoes smiled during the early 1960s festival.

Other Books by the Author

On the Way to Today, 1992
Holland, Michigan pictorial history

Holland Furnace Company, 1993
(Donald L. van Reken, co-author)

HOLLAND Happenings, Heroes & Hot Shots

Volume One 1994
Volume Two 1995
Volume Three 1996
Volume Four 1997

And Our Band Plays On 1995
(Donald L. van Reken, co-author)

Photo Credits

Randall P. Vande Water collection: 2 (3), 3 (1,5), 4, 5, 6 (2,3), 7, 8 (2,3,4), 9, 10, 13, 15 (2,3), 17, 18 (1,2,4), 20, 21, 23, 25 (2,3), 26, 27 (2,3,4), 28 (1,4), 29, (1,2,4), 30 (1,3,4), 31,(2,3,4,5), 33 (1), 34, 35, (1,2,3,5,6), 36 (1,2,4), 37 (1,2,3), 38 (1,2), 39 (3), 40 (1), 41 (1,2,4),42 (1), 45, 46 (1),. 47 (1,3), 48 (1), 49 (2),50, 52 (1,2,3), 54 (1,3,4), 55 (1,2), 56 (1,2,3,5), 57, 58 (1,3,4), 59, 60, 61 (2,3), 62, 63, 64 (1), 65, 66, 67, 68 (1), 69, 70, 71 (3,4) 72, 73 (1), 74 (1,3,4), 75, 76, 77, 78 (1,2,3), 79, 80, 81, 82, 83, 84 (1,2,3,5,) 85, 86, 89, 90 (1), 93 (2), 94 (3), 95 (2,4), 96, 98 (1,2), 99, 100, 101, 102, 103 (1), 104, 105, 106 (1), 107, 108, 109, 110, 111, 112, 113, 114, 115, 116, 117, 118 (2), 119 (1,3), 120 (1), 121.

Holland Sentinel: 2 (1,2), 10 (2), 11 (3), 13 (1), 14, 15 (1), 16 (2,4), 18 (3), 33 (3), 38 (3), 39 (4), 40 (1), 41 (4), 42 (5,2), 43, 44, 46 (2,3), 48 (2,3), 49 (3), 61 (1), 74 (2) 4?, 78 (1,3,4), 79 (2), 86, 87,88 (2), 91 (1,2,3), 92 (2), 93, 94 (1, 2), (1), 95 (1,3), 97, 103 (2), 106 (2), 118 (1), 120 (2,3).

Given to Randall P. Vande Water: 1, 3 (4), 10 (2), 12 (2), 13 (1), 14, 15 (1), 16 (2,4), 18 (3), 30 (2) ,32 (1), 39 (1,2), 47 (2), 49 (1), 54 (2) 55 (3),56, 58 (5), 64 (3), 92 (1)

Donald L. van Reken: 8(1), 24, 25 (1), 26 (2,3), 28 (2,3), 29 (3), 35 (4), 36 (3), 37 (4,5), 40 (2), 41 (3), 42 (3,4), 51, 52 (4), 53, 55 (2), 58 (2), 67 (3), 68 (2,3), 73 (2,3), 74 (2), 78 (4), 88 (1), 90 (2),

Holland Historical Trust: 3 (2), 19 (1,2,3), 64 (2), 84 (4).

Cover

R.P. Vande Water Collection: Photographed with a circuit camera, this wide-angle view of Lake Macatawa and the shoreline illustrates a panorama of Holland lake life in 1913. Mt. Pisgah is at far left. The Ottawa Beach Hotel, which burned Nov. 6, 1923, stands majestically at the left. The *City of Grand Rapids,* which sailed from Holland to Chicago, is in the center. Jenison Park is right center. The Lake Macatawa Bay basin is at far right. Note the Interurban loop in front of the Macatawa Hotel (not visible). The confectionary store is at right. Note the Model T autos, the sailboats and the Macatawa Bay Yacht Club clubhouse. Lookout Pavilion on the Incline Railroad is at far left.